ULTIMATE
FOOTBALL HEROES

MAGUIRE

FROM THE PLAYGROUND
TO THE PITCH

DINO

Published by Dino Books,
an imprint of John Blake Publishing,
2.25, The Plaza,
535 Kings Road,
Chelsea Harbour,
London SW10 0SZ

www.johnblakebooks.com

www.facebook.com/johnblakebooks
twitter.com/jblakebooks

First published in paperback in 2018

ISBN: 978 1 78946 047 6

British Library Cataloguing-in-Publication Data:

A catalogue record for this book is available from the British Library.

Design by www.envydesign.co.uk

Printed and bound in Great Britain by Clays Ltd, Elcograf S.p.A.

1 3 5 7 9 10 8 6 4 2

Papers used by John Blake Publishing are natural, recyclable products made from wood grown in sustainable forests. The manufacturing processes conform to the environmental regulations of the country of origin.

Every reasonable effort has been made to trace copyright-holders of material reproduced in this book, but if any have been inadvertently overlooked the publishers would be glad to hear from them.

John Blake Publishing is an imprint of Bonnier Books UK
www.bonnierbooks.co.uk

For all readers,
young and old(er)

ULTIMATE
FOOTBALL HEROES

Matt Oldfield is an accomplished writer and the editor-in-chief of football review site *Of Pitch & Page*. Tom Oldfield is a freelance sports writer and the author of biographies on Cristiano Ronaldo, Arsène Wenger and Rafael Nadal.

Cover illustration by Dan Leydon.
To learn more about Dan visit danleydon.com
To purchase his artwork visit etsy.com/shop/footynews
Or just follow him on Twitter @danleydon

TABLE OF CONTENTS

ACKNOWLEDGEMENTS

First of all, I'd like to thank John Blake Publishing – and particularly my editor James Hodgkinson – for giving me the opportunity to work on these books and for supporting me throughout. Writing stories for the next generation of football fans is both an honour and a pleasure.

I wouldn't be doing this if it wasn't for my brother Tom. I owe him so much and I'm very grateful for his belief in me as an author. I feel like Robin setting out on a solo career after a great partnership with Batman. I hope I do him (Tom, not Batman) justice with these new books.

Next up, I want to thank my friends for keeping

me sane during long hours in front of the laptop. Pang, Will, Mills, Doug, John, Charlie – the laughs and the cups of coffee are always appreciated.

I've already thanked my brother but I'm also very grateful to the rest of my family, especially Melissa, Noah and of course Mum and Dad. To my parents, I owe my biggest passions: football and books. They're a real inspiration for everything I do.

Finally, I couldn't have done this without Iona's encouragement and understanding during long, work-filled weekends. Much love to you.

CHAPTER 1

"SLABHEAD"
SAVES THE DAY!

Cosmos Arena, Samara, 7 July 2018

What a massive moment it was for Gareth
Southgate's young England team – they were about
to play in the 2018 World Cup quarter-finals! As
the players arrived at the Cosmos Arena, however,
they looked happy and relaxed. Harry Maguire had a
particularly big smile on his face. Why not? He was
in fantasy land!

In Summer 2014, Harry had just finished seventh
in League One with his hometown club, Sheffield
United.

In Summer 2015, he had just been relegated from
the Championship, while on loan at Wigan Athletic.

In Summer 2017, he had just been relegated from the Premier League with Hull City.

But now, in Summer 2018, Harry was an international footballer, starring for England at the World Cup!

The tournament had already been a big success for the team. They had beaten Tunisia, they had thrashed Panama and best of all, they had finally won a World Cup penalty shoot-out, against Colombia. Could they now go all the way and win the trophy? The players believed, and the fans believed too. England had gone football crazy once again!

It's coming home, it's coming home,
It's coming, FOOTBALL'S COMING HOME!

Every player was now a national hero, from goalkeeper Jordan Pickford all the way through to goal machine Harry Kane.

But perhaps the biggest heroes of all were Southgate's all-Yorkshire back three. Harry Maguire and Kyle Walker were both from Sheffield, while John Stones was born nearby in Barnsley. Kyle brought the speed, John brought the brains, and Harry brought the strength.

Each of them brought their own skill. Together, they formed a deadly defensive team. They were brilliant at the back, but also awesome in attack!

Harry was absolutely buzzing by the time the players arrived in the dressing room. After all, it wasn't every day that he got to play in a World Cup quarter-final! Sweden would be tough opponents but the new England were fearless. If they played well, they could beat anyone.

But wait, there was a problem! As Harry pulled on his red '6 MAGUIRE' shirt, it didn't fit. At six feet four, he was a big guy who needed a big shirt.

'Especially with that Slabhead of yours!' his England and Leicester teammate, Jamie Vardy, was always joking.

'Cheers, Vards!' Unfortunately for Harry, that nickname stuck. Now, lots of his teammates called him 'Slabhead' too.

With minutes to go before kick-off, the England's kit man, Pat, rushed off to print his name and number on a bigger shirt.

Some players might have panicked in that nerve-wracking situation, but not Harry. That wasn't his style. He was a laid-back lad, both on and off the pitch. He could handle the big-game pressure. In fact, he loved it. It was what being a professional footballer was all about.

'Thanks, Pat!' Harry shouted, quickly pulling on his new shirt. 'Right, let's win this, lads!'

It was still only his tenth cap but he was already one of the team leaders.

As usual, Harry started calmly, passing the ball around the defence, to Kyle and John, and to his left wing-back, Ashley. Southgate wanted his team to play out confidently from the back – that's why Harry was in the team!

For a big man, Harry was so comfortable on the ball. Whenever he spotted some space in front of him, he dribbled forward on the attack. With his skill and strength, it was so hard to stop him.

In the thirtieth minute, England won a corner-kick.

'Come on!' their fans cheered loudly in the stands. 'This is it!'

After lots of work in training, Southgate's side were now set-piece specialists. Every time the ball came into the box, they looked like they were going to score.

The deliveries were always dangerous, from Ashley on the left and Kieran Trippier on the right.

And the headers were always heroic, from John and from the two Harrys.

Earlier in the World Cup, in the last minute against Tunisia, Maguire had won the first header and Kane had scored the second. What could they do now against Sweden in the quarter-final?

As Ashley crossed from the left, Harry Maguire made his move towards the penalty spot. This ball was his, and no-one was going to stop him! He muscled his way past the Sweden defenders and powered a thumping header into the bottom corner.

Goooooooooooooooooooooaaaaaaaaaaaaaaaalllllllllllll llllllllllllll!!!!!!!!!!!!!!!!!!!!!

What a time to score his first-ever international goal! Harry raced towards the fans, pumping his fists and roaring like a lion. Playing for his country meant so much to him. Since his childhood, he had always been England's biggest fan. Now, he was England's goalscoring hero.

Down by the corner flag, Harry slid across the grass on his knees and his teammates piled on top of him.

'Yes, Slabhead!' John cheered.

'Slabhead, you beauty!' Kieran screamed.

As he got back to his feet, Harry looked up and listened. The delighted England fans were singing his song:

Harry Maguire, your defence is terrified!
Harry Maguire, na na na na na na na na na na!

What a feeling! Harry knew that his family would be singing along proudly. They were all there in Russia to cheer him on – his parents, Alan and Zoe, his brothers, Joe and Laurence, his sister Daisy, and his girlfriend, Fern. Without them, Harry's journey might never have happened.

And what a journey it had been! Harry had travelled with Joe and Laurence to watch England at Euro 2016. Just two years later, he was scoring in a World Cup quarter-final.

Harry couldn't get carried away, though.

'Focus!' Southgate shouted from the sidelines.

England had defending to do. Harry won header after header, and tackle after tackle. He certainly wasn't going to ruin his big match by making a big mistake.

In the second half, Jesse Lingard crossed to Dele Alli – 2–0 to England!

When the referee blew the final whistle, John jumped up into Harry's arms.

'We did it, Big Man – we're in the World Cup semi-finals!'

The England celebrations went on and on at the Cosmos Arena. The players partied on the pitch, right in front of their loyal fans. They were all staying in Russia, but as for football itself:

It's coming home, it's coming home,
It's coming, FOOTBALL'S COMING HOME!

'Slabhead saves the day!' Jamie cheered, giving Harry a big hug. He was so pleased for his friend and teammate.

'Cheers, Vards. I wouldn't be here if it wasn't for your annoying banter!'

It took a little while for the importance of their victory to sink in. England hadn't reached the World Cup semi-finals since 1990. That was twenty-eight years ago!

It wasn't just that, though. With their spirit and style, the players had made their country so proud. Back at the base camp, Harry watched all the amazing videos of the celebrations at home in England.

'Wow, look how happy we've made everyone!' he thought to himself.

Harry's face was all over the Internet, and it was even tattooed on a fan's chest!

At the age of twenty-five, Harry had already

achieved his childhood dreams and more. Not only had he become a top Premier League player, but now he was also an England World Cup hero. 'England World Cup hero' – would he ever get used to the sound of those words?

It hadn't been an easy road to glory, however. Harry had worked his way up, step by step, level by level, game after game.

It had taken years of dedication, determination, and brotherly battles.

It had taken years of support from family, friends and coaches.

But boy, had it all been worth it!

CHAPTER 2

BROTHERLY BATTLES

Growing up, Joe and Harry were as inseparable as brothers can be. Where one young Maguire went, the other one almost always followed. Joe was older by eighteen months but that never stopped Harry. Anything his brother could do, he could do too – walking, reading, riding a bike and, of course, playing football.

Their dad, Alan, had been a good player when he was younger. He was now a coach at the local club in Sheffield, Brunsmeer Athletic, and he got his sons kicking as soon as he could.

'That's it!' Alan shouted as Joe booted the ball towards goal. With a dramatic dive, he let his son's shot roll right past him and into the net. *GOAL!*

'Yes!' Joe cheered, lifting his shirt over his head just like he'd seen the superstars do on TV.

'Right, your turn, Harry.'

Anything his brother could do, he could do too, only better! Harry was so determined. As he stood there between the goalposts, Alan could see a very serious look on his younger son's little face.

Harry took a really long run-up, swung his right leg back as far as it would go, and then *Bang!* He booted the ball into the air and it landed perfectly in the bottom corner. *GOAL!*

'What a strike!' his dad cried out with a shocked look on his face. He hadn't even bothered with his usual dramatic dive. How had Harry done that? He was still only four years old!

'Yes!' Harry cheered, sliding across the mud on his knees.

Joe watched on with a sulky frown. He wasn't going to let his younger brother take all the glory. 'Right, it's my turn again!' he said sternly.

Hours later, Alan was still standing there between

the goalposts as his sons took shots at goal, over and over again.

As they got older, the Maguire brothers became more and more competitive. They battled over school reports, pocket money, TV shows and, of course, football.

'Boys, that's enough!' their mum, Zoe, would shout whenever they dared to play one vs one in the living room. 'You know the rules – go outside if you want to do that!'

In their back garden, Joe and Harry didn't have to worry about breaking vases, or tripping over table legs. They were free to play, and play hard.

'Let the battle begin!' Joe said, grinning like an evil villain.

He was bigger and stronger than Harry, and he often used that to his advantage. Fouls? In their back-garden games, there was no such thing! They could do as many pushes, pulls, shoulder barges and sliding tackles as they liked.

After all, there were no referees in their brotherly battles – just parents ready to step in if they really started fighting.

'Play nicely out there, okay?'

'Yes, Mum!'

Harry loved every minute of it. Yes, he was smaller, but he was more skilful than his brother. He was a natural with the ball at his feet. He knew that he could dribble past Joe, and if only he could dodge his angry arms and long legs, then... *GOAL!*

Harry was also braver. He hated losing, and especially losing to his elder brother. That was the worst thing in the world! Joe would boast about it for days. So, Harry always did everything he could to make sure that didn't happen.

He chased, he challenged,

He barged, he blocked.

Their battles were always close and always fierce. They couldn't help it; they were competitive kids who loved football.

'Sorry!' they called out when they smashed a kitchen window.

'Sorry!' they called out when they turned the garden into a mud-bath and their dad had to lay down new grass.

Sometimes, their battles went on all day long and then carried on the next morning too. However long it took, they always ended with red faces, red knees and sweaty shirts.

'Well played,' Harry said, shaking Joe's hand. He was tired but happy because he had another victory to add to his list. 'Another battle tomorrow?'

'Of course,' his brother replied immediately. 'I want revenge!'

Harry and Joe's one vs one battles later turned into two vs two. Laurence wanted to do everything his older brothers did, and so did their sister, Daisy. With double the players, there was double the trouble.

It was total mayhem in the Maguire back garden, with tackles flying in everywhere. Their dad's freshly-laid grass didn't stand a chance.

'Why are our kids so competitive?' Zoe asked, as she kept watch from the window. 'I don't know where they get it from!'

Alan smiled fondly. 'Oh, I think I know. Sorry!'

CHAPTER 3

BRUNSMEER ATHLETIC

As much as Harry loved his brotherly battles with Joe, they did get a little boring after a while. It was the same challenge, every time! There were so many other opponents out there for Harry to compete with. Plus, how fun would it be to finally play *with* Joe, rather than against him?

'Dad, when can I come and play for Brunsmeer?' Harry begged. 'Please!'

When he was younger, Alan had been Brunsmeer Athletic's big, powerful centre-back, but now he was their Under-11s coach. Joe was already in the team and when Harry turned eight years old, he was finally allowed to join him. He was at least a year younger than everyone else, but that never stopped Harry. Anything his brother could do, he could do too.

Joe was a strong defender, just like his dad. Harry, however, was a different type of player. He wasn't as big as the rest of his family and he was more comfortable on the ball. He loved dribbling and passing his way towards goal.

'Right, we'll play you in centre midfield,' Alan decided before he had even trained with the team.

Harry would have played anywhere, but centre midfield was the best position on the pitch. He still got to battle bravely for the ball, just like he did in the back garden at home. But on top of that, he also got to rush forward and use his skills to attack.

'It's the best of both worlds!' he told Joe happily.

Harry loved wearing Brunsmeer's red and black stripes. Every Sunday morning, he woke up bright and early, buzzing for the match ahead. The weather, the pitch, the opponents – none of that really mattered to him. Harry just wanted to play and have fun. When it came to football, he was totally fearless.

'Bring it on!' he shouted in wind, rain or sunshine.

Harry was like a busy bee, buzzing all over the pitch. He treated every match like a brotherly battle that he could not lose. *Tackle! Block! Header! Interception!*

'Great work, bro!' Joe called out again and again.

But once Harry was on the ball, everything slowed down. Now that he had it, he didn't want to waste it. If he could see a teammate in space, he played the simple pass, but if not, he held on to it and dribbled forward. He made it look so easy. He wasn't the quickest player around but it was so hard to get the ball off him.

'The Maguire Boys' were soon the talk of the Sheffield youth leagues. With Joe controlling the back and Harry bossing the midfield, Brunsmeer were unbeatable.

Harry and Joe were the deadliest duo around. When they played together for their primary school team, the game was over before it even started. Their opponents didn't stand a chance!

Parents would ask:

'How did you get on?'

'We lost 12–0!'

'12–0? Who were we playing against?'

'Immaculate Conception.'

'Were the Maguire Boys playing?'

'Yes, both of them.'

'That explains it then!'

Alan was very proud of his sons but he never gave them special star treatment. In fact, quite the opposite – as they got older, he expected more from them than from anyone else in the team.

'You're a lot better than that,' he would tell Harry whenever he had a poor game. 'Your passing was sloppy today and you were totally off the pace!'

At first, the criticism hurt but Harry knew that his dad was just trying to help him improve as a footballer. Everyone made mistakes; everyone had a bad day every now and again. He just had to believe in himself and keep getting better.

'If you keep learning and working hard, you could all be professional footballers one day,' Alan said to his three sons. The youngest, Laurence, was now following in his brothers' footsteps. He believed in them.

'A professional footballer!' Harry repeated to himself excitedly. That was his dream, but could it *really* be more than just a dream? With lots of hard work, he hoped so.

CHAPTER 4

WORLD CUP 2002

'Morning, Harry!' Mrs Emmot, the Immaculate Conception Primary Headmistress called out as she walked past the assembly hall.

Harry tore his eyes away from the big screen for long enough to turn and reply politely, 'Morning, Miss!'

'So, are England finally going to win the World Cup again?' she asked.

'Of course, Miss!' he nodded eagerly.

Harry had only been five years old for the 1998 tournament, so 2002 was his first proper World Cup, and he was loving it! Every day, there were more exciting international football matches to watch –

France vs Senegal, Brazil vs China, Cameroon vs Germany, Mexico vs Italy…

'This is the best thing ever!' Harry cheered. It was a non-stop football fiesta.

The 2002 World Cup was taking place in Japan and South Korea. They were eight hours ahead of English time, which meant that the 3.30pm kick-offs were shown at 7.30am for Harry in Chesterfield. Perfect – he could watch the matches on a big screen in the assembly hall before the school day started!

Harry watched, Harry learned and Harry dreamed. How amazing would it be to become one of the best players on the planet! 'The Maguire Boys' were the stars of the local school tournaments but one day, they could be World Cup stars. Anything was possible!

Although Harry watched as many World Cup matches as he could, the team he was really supporting was England. The nation had high hopes for Sven-Göran Eriksson's team. With Michael Owen up front, David Beckham in midfield, and Sol Campbell in defence, why couldn't the Three Lions go all the way?

Harry was still playing in central midfield for his club and for his school, but his favourite England player was the young centre-back, Rio Ferdinand.

Ferdinand was a cool new kind of defender. He was still awesome at tackling, heading and marking strikers, but he was also awesome at passing. When he got the ball in defence, he didn't panic and hoof the ball up the pitch like some centre-backs. Instead, Ferdinand was calm, classy and confident.

'Apparently, he was an attacker when he was younger,' Harry's dad told him.

Of course! That made total sense to Harry. Hopefully, if he grew big and tall, he could be the next Rio Ferdinand...

Against England's old rivals Argentina, it was Beckham who stepped up and scored a penalty under so much pressure. 1–0!

In the second half, however, it was Ferdinand's turn to be the hero. As hard as Argentina's star striker Gabriel Batistuta tried, he just couldn't get through! In the Immaculate Conception assembly hall, Harry cheered every block and every clearance.

When the final whistle blew, he punched the air.

'What a win!'

Harry got even more excited during England's Round of 16 match against Denmark. In the fifth minute, Beckham curled a corner to the back-post and Ferdinand headed the ball over the goal line. 1–0! While Rio danced on the pitch in Japan, Harry danced at his school in Chesterfield.

'England! England!' he chanted with his friends.

Owen made it 2–0 and Emile Heskey made it 3–0. The Three Lions were through to the World Cup quarter-finals!

At 7.30am on Friday, 21 June, the Immaculate Conception assembly hall was packed for the massive match against Brazil. Harry was England's biggest fan and he wanted them to win so badly. He was too nervous to even eat.

'You do know you're not playing in the game, right?' Joe joked.

Very funny! Harry rolled his eyes at his brother but in his head, he was thinking, 'How amazing would it be if I *was* playing in a World Cup quarter-final?'

That dream would have to wait. For now, he was cheering on Ferdinand, Beckham and co. When Owen scored, Harry jumped for joy. 1–0 – England were beating Brazil!

Sadly, it couldn't last. Just before half-time, Ronaldinho dribbled through the defence and passed to Rivaldo. 1–1!

'Come on, England!' Harry shouted up at the screen.

Early in the second half, Brazil won a free kick way out on the right wing. Ronaldinho placed the ball down and looked up at the England goal.

'No way, he can't shoot from there!' Harry said to his friends. 'He's going to cross it.'

But the ball sailed over David Seaman's arm and into the top corner. 2–1!

Harry's young heart sank. What a disaster! The England players kept going but they couldn't grab a second goal. Their World Cup was over.

'What a fluke!' Harry muttered moodily. 'There's no way Ronaldinho meant to do that.'

After a few days of disappointment, Harry went

back to watching the semi-finals on the big screen at school. Even though his favourite player and favourite team were out, he could still learn lots from players like Ronaldo and Germany's Michael Ballack.

Harry would never forget the 2002 World Cup. By the end of that special month, he knew what his life-long dream would be – to one day play for England at a major international tournament.

CHAPTER 5

THE BOY'S A BLADE!

In Sheffield, there are two big football teams: Sheffield Wednesday and Sheffield United. The clubs are fierce rivals, so it's important to choose your colours carefully – blue and white for Wednesday, or red and white for United.

Harry had a very difficult decision to make. His dad was a Wednesday fan but his mum supported United! Which team would Harry pick? Would he become an Owl or a Blade?

Alan did his best to persuade his son. He took Harry to matches at Wednesday's big Hillsborough stadium.

'See?' his dad turned to him as the crowd clapped

and cheered loudly. 'This is the team to support, son!'

Harry loved the loud atmosphere at Hillsborough but the football was hard to watch. Wednesday seemed to lose every single match they played! When Harry was ten years old, in 2003, they got relegated from the First Division to the Second Division.

'You should have seen us back in 1997,' his dad said, trying to stay positive. 'Wednesday finished seventh in the Premier League! We'll be back there soon, I'm sure.'

United, meanwhile, were flying high. With Rob Page in defence, Michael Brown in midfield and Carl Asaba and Paul Peschisolido in attack, the Blades finished third in the First Division. That was a massive nineteen places higher than Wednesday! United were even one match away from promotion to the Premier League but they sadly they lost to Wolves in the play-off final.

'Never mind,' his mum sighed. 'There's always next year!'

Despite that disappointment, Harry decided that supporting United looked a lot more fun than supporting Wednesday. Plus, by the age of eleven, he had another very special reason for wearing red and white. After a year at Barnsley, Harry had been scouted by the Sheffield United youth academy.

'Sorry, Dad, I'm a Blade now!' he announced proudly. He had the club kit to prove it.

It didn't take long for Alan to also become a Blades fan. If he wanted to support his son, what else could he do?

Life at Sheffield United was a dream come true for Harry. It was exactly the kind of challenge he had been looking for. He loved competing with top players and training under top coaches.

'I'm learning so much!' Harry told his dad happily at dinner.

'Hey, what are you saying about my sessions at Brunsmeer?' Alan joked.

Wearing his team tracksuit, Harry couldn't help dreaming of the future. In five years' time, he could be playing for the Under-18s, then the reserves, then the Sheffield United first team. In ten years' time, he could be a Bramall Lane hero!

'One step at a time,' he had to keep reminding himself.

Unfortunately, Harry's next step wasn't becoming Sheffield United's first-ever twelve-year-old wonderkid. Instead, he became one of the club's ball boys at Bramall Lane.

'Ball boy? What a boring job!' his younger brother, Laurence, argued but Harry loved it, even on the wettest, coldest winter nights.

At every Sheffield United home game, Harry got to watch the senior players in action, right from the side of the pitch. They were so close that he could reach out and touch them! Sometimes, he *did* touch them when he handed them the ball for a throw-in.

'Keith Gillespie smiled at me,' Harry told Laurence, 'and he even said thanks!'

Suddenly, ball boy sounded like a pretty awesome job, in fact.

Harry's stool next to the pitch was one of the best seats in the whole Bramall Lane stadium, especially during the 2006–07 season, because The Blades were playing in the Premier League!

So, Harry could not only watch Sheffield United stars Phil Jagielka and Rob Hulse, but also:

Chelsea's John Terry and Didier Drogba...

...Manchester United's Rio Ferdinand and Cristiano Ronaldo...

...Liverpool's Xabi Alonso and Steven Gerrard...

...and Arsenal's Cesc Fàbregas and Thierry Henry.

Harry was in fantasy land! It was an amazing opportunity to study superstar footballers up close. Their decision-making, their movement, their vision, their teamwork. Harry tried to take in as much as he could. He wanted every game to go on forever.

Even after Sheffield United were relegated back to the First Division, Harry carried on being a ball boy in the Championship. There was still plenty for him to watch and learn from players like Ryan Shawcross at Stoke City and Kevin Phillips at West Brom.

It was those Premier League glory days, however, that made Harry more determined than ever. He had a new target to aim for. With hard work and self-belief, Harry would lead The Blades back to the big-time.

CHAPTER 6

MR SPORTY

Although football was Harry's favourite thing in the world, he loved playing all sports. Anything that involved running and competing, he would say 'I'm in!' immediately. He always wanted to win, even if there was no trophy.

When he enrolled at St Mary's Roman Catholic High School, he had a wide range of options. Harry quickly showed his new PE teacher, Mr McKee, that he was an excellent all-round sportsman.

Harry ran the 800 metres,

he threw the heavy discus,

he joined the school's successful cross-country team,

he played golf,

he played tennis,

he played badminton,

he played rugby,

he played hockey...

The list went on and on and on.

'Is there any sport that you're not good at?' Mr McKee joked.

Harry smiled cheekily. 'I'm not much of a gymnast, Sir. I can barely do a forward roll!'

'Well, we'll see about that, Maguire!'

When Harry decided that he wanted to achieve something, he worked really, really hard until he achieved it. He took that same can-do attitude with his school subjects too.

'Your determination will get you far in life!' his deputy headteacher told him when he got his GCSE results aged sixteen. He had got 3 A*s, 4 As and a B. His parents were delighted and so were his brothers, although they didn't always show it.

'What happened with that B, clever clogs?' Joe teased.

'Shhh you!' their mum laughed. 'We're so proud of you, son! What's next – college?'

Harry's parents had always let him play as much sport as he wanted, just as long as it didn't get in the way of his schoolwork. Education was very important for them, and for Harry's future.

'You've got to keep concentrating on your studies,' his mum told him when he was fourteen. 'There are hundreds of young players there at the academy, and most of them are not going to make it as professional footballers. You're a bright boy, so make sure you've got a Plan B!'

Harry had listened to his parents. He had the good grades he needed to go to college, but he was still playing for the Sheffield United youth team and hoping to have a long career at the club. He liked Maths but he *loved* football!

In between all the other sports, Harry had still found time to shine for the St Mary's football team. He was their midfield maestro, controlling games with his passing and dribbling. Once the battle started, no opponent could stop him.

'Once you get out on the pitch, it's like you double in size or something,' his best friend Danny joked. 'Maybe you're a superhero!'

Harry had proved that he was an excellent all-round sportsman, but football was his natural talent. With his perfect mix of passion and technique, he made the beautiful game look so easy.

'You've got what it takes to get to the top,' his PE teacher Mr McKee told him again and again. 'Whatever you do, don't give up on your dream!'

Mr McKee didn't really need to tell him, though. No-one was more determined than Harry. It was time to focus fully on football. Some of his friends thought he should have done that a lot earlier, but Harry disagreed. Over time, he had learned different skills from each of his different sports:

Cross-country gave him the stamina to run for even longer on the football pitch.

Rugby improved his bravery, and his dribbling skills too. If he could weave through tackles with a ball in his hand, he could do it with a ball at his feet too!

Hockey helped to develop his passing abilities and his vision on the ball. That was really important in football as well.

'See? It's all part of my training!' Harry argued.

Now, though, it was time for Mr Sporty to become Mr Football.

CHAPTER 7

THE PERFECT POSITION

By the time he turned sixteen, Harry knew that
he was going to become a professional footballer.
His family knew it, his friends knew it – even the
Sheffield United youth coaches knew it. There
were two important questions, however, that still
needed to be answered:

1) Was Harry good enough to play for Sheffield
   United? And...

2) What position would Harry play?

The first question could wait but the second
couldn't because all of a sudden, Harry was growing
taller and taller each day. He shot up into the sky –

six feet tall, six feet one, six feet two. . . all the way up to six feet four!

'Blimey, kid, what have you been eating lately?' the Sheffield United youth coaches asked in awe as they looked up at him.

Since his very first game for Brunsmeer, Harry had been a busy central midfielder, full of energy and skill. But now that he was a giant, could he still play that role? He wasn't so quick and nimble anymore. With longer legs, he felt so clumsy on the ball.

'Where do you want to be in three years' time?' the academy manager, John Pemberton, asked him during an important meeting in his office.

Harry knew the answer to that one. 'I want to be playing for the first team,' he replied confidently.

'Well, I'm sorry but I don't think you'll make it in midfield,' Pemberton told him. He had a plan, though: 'Let's see what you can do in defence instead.'

If it would help the team, Harry was happy to try anything. Just as long as he played professional football, he didn't mind *where* he played on the pitch.

'Welcome to the family position!' Joe chuckled. He

was a centre-back, their dad was a centre-back, their brother Laurence was a centre-back, and now Harry was too.

'Thanks,' Harry replied. 'I think I'm going to need your help!'

Zonal marking, offside traps, clever strikers – it was a whole new world for Harry to get used to. Fortunately, he was a fast learner and he had great teammates and coaches to help him.

'That's it – show them who's boss!' the academy manager shouted as Harry jumped highest to win a header. He was so competitive that he hated losing a single battle.

The ball flew through the air, over the halfway line, and landed at the feet of United's striker.

'Blimey, that big head of yours is more powerful than your boot!' Harry's centre-back partner, Terry Kennedy, laughed.

Pemberton was delighted with the youngster's progress. Harry could read the game so well for a young player and get himself into the right positions to deal with any danger. He was starting to look like he'd been a defender all his life. It was time for Stage Two of the master plan.

'Maguire, go short for the pass!' Pemberton called out as the goalkeeper got ready to kick the ball downfield.

Harry had the height and strength of a centre-back but he could pass and dribble like a midfielder. That made him a very rare talent and Pemberton wanted to make the most of him.

When the goalkeeper rolled it to him, Harry just hoofed the ball long straight away. He couldn't take risks so close to his own goal. He was a defender now! His coach, however, had other ideas.

'Take your time on the ball,' Pemberton urged. 'Play like you used to play in midfield. Don't worry if you make a few mistakes.'

At first, Harry made lots of mistakes.

Sometimes, when the strikers pressed him, he panicked and played a bad pass, either too short or too heavy. *GOAL!*

'Sorry!'

Sometimes, he tried to dribble past one opponent too many and got tackled. *GOAL!*

'Sorry!'

Whatever the reason, Pemberton always said the same thing. 'Head up, keep going!'

Harry hated giving away goals. It left a horrible sinking feeling in his stomach. His teammates didn't say anything but they didn't have to. Harry knew that it was all his fault. He was letting his team down badly.

'But I'm just doing what I'm told!' he argued with himself. His manager had told him to be bold on the ball.

Harry had to persevere and he had to improve. Thanks to lots of hard work in training, he soon looked his usual, comfortable self again. And Harry's skills became Sheffield United's secret weapon.

Under pressure in their own half? No problem! Harry would bring the ball out of defence, weaving his way up the pitch and then picking out a pass.

1–0 down, with a few minutes to go? No problem! Harry moved forward confidently, looking for the chance to shoot.

'Congratulations, kid,' Pemberton smiled. 'You've found your perfect position!'

CHAPTER 8

FA YOUTH CUP

There was no stopping Harry, now that he had found his perfect position. He couldn't wait to test himself against England's best young strikers in the 2011 FA Youth Cup.

'Let the battles begin!' Harry and Terry cheered together.

Could anyone defeat Yorkshire's deadliest defensive duo? It didn't seem so:

Cheltenham Town 1–4 Sheffield United
Sheffield United 3–0 Millwall
Sheffield United 3–1 Blackpool
Leicester City 1–2 Sheffield United

With four wins in a row, the young Blades were
through to the semi-finals.

'Great work, lads,' Pemberton cheered proudly.
'Two more performances like that and we'll be in the
final!'

Sheffield United had never got that far in the sixty
years of the FA Youth Cup. Could these kids make
history? The club's fans were delighted to have
something to cheer about. Their senior team was
struggling down at the bottom of the First Division.

United! United! United!

Mark Smith, the Reserves coach, gave Harry some
very good news. 'Speedo is really impressed with
you. Keep it up, kid!'

Gary Speed, the Sheffield United manager, had
watched him play? Wow, Harry was now even more
determined to dazzle in defence!

A few days after his eighteenth birthday, he
travelled to Villa Park to take on Aston Villa. Ahead
of the biggest game of his football career, Harry felt
more excited than nervous. Harry believed in himself
and he believed in all of his brilliant teammates.

Together, they could handle the pressure and win yet another battle.

'Let's keep it tight tonight,' Pemberton told them in the dressing room before kick-off. 'Remember, we've got the home leg back at Bramall Lane still to come.'

The young Blades wanted to win both games, though. Harry and Terry at the back were stopping every Villa attack. What could Sheffield United do on the counter-attack? Just before half-time, Jordan Slew dribbled into the Villa box and cut the ball back for Joe Ironside to score. 1–0!

Watching from the halfway line, Harry punched the air with joy. Now, he had more defending to do.

A long ball over the top… no problem! Harry calmly let it run through to his goalkeeper.

A cross into the box… no problem! With his big head, Harry cleared the danger.

A long-range shot… no problem! Harry bravely blocked it with his body.

When the final whistle blew, he punched the air again, this time with both fists. A win *and* a cleansheet – what a perfect late birthday present!

'We're halfway there, lads,' Pemberton said, patting them all on the back.

In the second leg, Sheffield United scored, again just before half-time. This time, though, the goal was created by their dazzling defenders. Harry crossed from the left to Terry at the back post. He headed it down for Elliott Whitehouse to tap in. 2–0 on aggregate!

Harry joined in the team celebrations and then ran back to his own half. He had more defending to do.

A Villa shot from the edge of the area... no problem! Harry blocked it with his long legs.

Another long-range Villa shot... no problem! Harry headed the ball away.

What a hero! At the final whistle, he threw his arms up above his head and hugged Terry. Two big games, two big clean sheets.

'We did it!' Harry shouted. 'We're in the final!'

It was already one of Sheffield United's greatest ever achievements, but could the young Blades go all the way and win the trophy? It wasn't going to be easy. Their final opponents would be Premier League giants, Manchester United. The club had already won the FA Youth Cup nine times, most famously with their Class of 1992, featuring David Beckham, Ryan Giggs, Paul Scholes, Gary Neville, Phil Neville and Nicky Butt.

Nineteen years on, their Class of 2011 was packed with future superstars too, including a young midfield maestro called Paul Pogba.

'We've got nothing to be scared of tonight,' Pemberton told his players before the first leg at Bramall Lane. 'We deserve to be here, so let's show them what we can do!'

It was going to be Harry's biggest test yet. Jesse Lingard, Ravel Morrison and Will Keane were all excellent and promising young attackers at Manchester United with lots of speed, skill and clever movement.

'Come on, this is going to have to be our best game ever!' Harry told Terry as they took up their positions on the pitch.

Unfortunately, with 30,000 fans watching, Harry's night quickly became a nightmare.

As Pogba crossed from the right wing, Lingard slipped away from Harry and got to the ball first. His shot deflected up off the goalkeeper and struck the crossbar. As it bounced down, Harry tried to clear it but instead, he could only head the ball into his own net. 1–0 to Manchester United!

What a disaster! Harry had that horrible sinking feeling in his stomach again. He had let his team down. He wanted to hide away but he couldn't.

'Head up, keep going!' – that's what his coach always told him. Harry stayed strong and fought until the final whistle.

'Well done, kid,' Pemberton said, putting an arm around Harry's broad shoulders. With a 2–2 draw, Sheffield United's FA Youth Cup dream was still alive. 'You showed real guts out there.'

In the second leg at Old Trafford, the young Blades did their best, but ultimately Manchester United were just too good. Morrison and Keane scored two goals each in a 4–1 thrashing.

No, Sheffield United hadn't won, but Harry was still really proud of his runners-up medal. The FA Youth Cup final had taught him some tough lessons about football at the highest level. Harry still had a long way to go and lots to learn, but he was on the right track.

CHAPTER 9

FIRST GAME FOR THE FIRST TEAM

By April 2011, the Sheffield United manager, Micky Adams, was under real pressure. The Blades were about to get relegated down to League One, and the fans were furious. They booed the team's most experienced players, shouting,

'Get them off, they don't deserve to wear the shirt!'

What did the fans want Adams to do instead?

'Give the kids a chance!' they demanded.

The juniors had just reached the FA Youth Cup final, after all. They couldn't do any worse than the seniors.

Who should Adams choose? Elliott? Joe? Jordan?

Terry? No, Harry was the team's stand-out player and not just because of his height. He also had that amazing mix of passion and talent. It was time to see if he was ready for the Championship challenge.

When Harry first started training with the first team, some of the senior players were shocked. They took one look at him and thought, 'No way, that kid's too big to be a good footballer!'

That all changed, though, when Harry got the ball. With a neat first touch, he dribbled forward from the back, gliding past one player and then another. With great composure, he looked up and played a clever pass through to the striker. Wow! Sheffield United's senior players were *really* shocked now!

'Ok, that kid can *play!*' they said, having all changed their minds.

Harry didn't play in the home game against Leeds United but he was there on the subs bench just in case. It was like the good old days of being a ball boy at Bramall Lane. From up close, he could watch Sheffield United's centre-back Nyron Nosworthy really carefully.

How tightly did he mark the Leeds strikers? How often did he talk to the other defenders?

Harry was always looking to learn. He had come a long way since those ball boy days and he was now so close to achieving his childhood dream. So close that he could almost reach out and touch it.

Harry's whole family was there at the stadium, hoping to see him make his debut.

'You'll get your chance soon,' his mum reassured him after the match.

She was right. Harry was back on the bench for the home game against Cardiff City and this time, he didn't stay there.

Sheffield United were heading towards another disastrous defeat. They were losing 1–0 early in the second half, when not one but two defenders got injured! First Nyron hobbled off, and then Joe Mattock. Nick Montgomery came on for Nyron, but who would Adams bring on to replace Joe? Harry's heart was beating extra fast on the bench.

'Maguire, you ready?' one of the coaches called out.

Harry nodded eagerly. Of course, he was ready!
He jumped up out of his seat and tucked in his red
and white shirt on the touchline. '40 MAGUIRE,'
the back of it read. This was it – his first game for the
Sheffield United first team.

'Just take your time and keep it simple,' his
manager Micky Adams told him. 'Good luck!'

The Sheffield United fans clapped and cheered as
Harry ran onto the field. Finally, Adams was listening
to them, and giving the kids a chance. The mood
lifted around Bramall Lane.

'They reckon this guy's going to be the next John
Terry!'

'He's a future England captain, I heard, and he's a
local lad too.'

Harry was determined to make a good first
impression and live up to those great expectations.
He was playing against Craig Bellamy, one of the best
and smartest strikers in the league. The Welshman
had scored eighty-one Premier League goals for clubs
like Manchester City and Liverpool.

What a big first test for Harry! As he took a deep

breath, the words of his youth coach flashed through his head – 'Show them who's boss!'

He was ready for battle. When the first pass arrived at Bellamy's feet, BOOM! Harry won the ball with a tough tackle that sent Bellamy flying through the air.

'That's more like it!' The Sheffield United supporters rose to their feet to clap and cheer their new young star. 'I love him already!'

Slowly, Bellamy got back to his feet. He accepted Harry's handshake and smiled. 'Boy, you're a big lad! Is that why they brought you on?'

After that very strong start, however, Harry nearly went from hero to villain. United passed the ball across the defence, just like Pemberton had always encouraged the youth team to do. That style was perfect for Harry but just as it came to him, he slipped and fell. *GASP!* The fans feared the worst but fortunately, Cardiff didn't score a second goal.

Phew! Harry breathed a sigh of relief.

'Forget that, keep going!' Neill Collins, his centre-back partner, told him.

Harry focused on his task and fought hard until the final whistle. The match ended in another defeat for Sheffield United but at least the game had brought one bright light at the end of the dark tunnel: Harry.

He walked all the way around the stadium, thanking the fans for their amazing support. He wanted to stay on the pitch and keep playing.

'Great performance, kid,' Adams said as Harry finally made his way down the tunnel to the dressing room.

Upstairs in the players' lounge, his family was waiting to congratulate him too.

'Well done, I'm so proud of you!' his mum said, hugging him tightly.

'Yes but we lost,' Harry reminded her. 'Again.'

'You played so brilliantly, though. Could you hear everyone cheering when you made that big tackle?'

'Could you hear everyone groaning when you nearly gave away that goal?' his brother Laurence added cheekily.

Sheffield United only had five games left in the Championship season. Harry started four of them and even won the man of the match award against Preston. He would have started the other game too, if he hadn't been suspended.

The suspension happened in a game against Bristol City, Nick tried to pass the ball back to Harry but instead, it fell to the striker. Harry panicked and brought him down. *Foul!* The referee gave Bristol City a penalty and sent Harry off.

'Nooooo! Why did I dive in like that?' he groaned as he slowly jogged off the pitch. The horrible sinking feeling was back.

That red card helped to keep Harry's feet firmly on the ground. He couldn't get too big for his big boots. Yes, he was now a Sheffield United first-team star and a fans' favourite, but he still had lots more to learn.

CHAPTER 10

LIFE IN LEAGUE ONE

And what better place to learn than in League One?
That's where Sheffield United would be playing for the
2011–12 season. During the summer, Harry's centre
back partner, Neill, passed on some helpful advice.

'Look, I know you like to get the ball down and
pass it around, but you're playing a different kind
of football now. In League One, it's much more
physical. Teams are going to hoof long balls up to
their big, strong strikers, who will to try to push you
around. Just be ready for that.'

'Thanks, I will be!'

Harry didn't mind playing dirty if he had to. He
was six feet four, after all!

On the opening day of the season, Sheffield United

travelled to Oldham Athletic. Their striker, Matt Smith, was even taller than Harry – he was six feet six!

'See!' Neill said with a smile. 'Welcome to League One!'

Luckily, Harry loved nothing more than a challenge. He didn't win every header but he did keep Smith quiet.

Early in the second half, Harry went forward for a corner-kick. The penalty area was like a wrestling ring, with lots of pushing and shoving everywhere. But when the cross came in, Harry outmuscled and then outjumped his marker to power a header into the top corner.

Goooooooooooooooooooaaaaaaaaaaaaaaaaalllllllllllll llllllllllllllll!!!!!!!!!!!!!!!!!!!!!

It was the moment Harry had dreamt about since he was eleven years old – his first goal for Sheffield United! He watched the ball land in the back of the net and then ran over to the away fans to celebrate. He lept high into the air and then dropped to his knees. It was the greatest feeling ever.

Neill was one of the first teammates to hug Harry.

'Ok fine, you're ready for League One!' he joked.

Sheffield United started the season well with four wins out of five, and three clean sheets. Thanks to Harry, they had the best defence in the division.

The team's new manager, Danny Wilson, was delighted. Young players usually made a few mistakes, especially centre-backs. But at the age of eighteen, Harry already looked just as calm and consistent as an experienced pro like Neill.

But would Sheffield United be able to hold on to their star centre-back for long? Hopefully, for as long as the club got promoted back up to the Championship.

The Blades spent the whole season in the top six but in the end, they finished third, three points behind their bitter rivals, Sheffield Wednesday.

'Hey, it's not over yet,' Wilson told his disappointed players. 'We just have to win the play-offs now!'

There was good news to help cheer Harry up. He was one of three United players named in the League One Team of the Year. Not bad for a nineteen-year-old playing in League One for the first time! It was a very proud moment but Harry kept his eyes on the prize – promotion through the play-offs.

With a tense 1–0 win over Stevenage, Sheffield United were through to the final. As a local lad, Harry was especially excited. Two years earlier, he had been a youth player and a ball boy. Now, he was about to play in a final at Wembley Stadium. Everything was happening so fast but somehow, Harry stayed as calm as ever.

'We know Huddersfield will be a tough team,' he told the media, 'but we have always believed that we will be in the Championship next season.'

As Harry walked out onto the pitch, he looked up at the 52,000 cheering fans. The atmosphere was amazing and the game hadn't even kicked off yet.

'I could get used to playing in front of a crowd like this!' he chuckled to himself.

Pressure? Harry loved pressure! It was what being a top professional footballer was all about. He couldn't wait for the biggest battle of his life to begin.

'Come on, let's do this!' he cheered.

Sadly, it wasn't the fun final that both sets of fans

were hoping for. Instead, it was tight and tense.
Neither team was brave enough to take a risk, in
case they made a mistake. After 120 minutes without
a goal, the match went all the way to penalties.

'At least that's another clean sheet for us!' Harry
joked, trying to lighten the mood. Neill was taking one
of Sheffield's five penalties and he looked nervous.

Both teams hugged their goalkeepers and wished
them luck. Who would be the hero? United's Steve
Simonsen, or Huddersfield's Alex Smithies?

After ten penalties, the score was 2–2. The shoot out
went to sudden death, and even Harry was starting to
feel a little anxious. One miss and it would be all over.

3–2 to Huddersfield, 3–3, 4–3 to Huddersfield...

It was Harry's turn to take a penalty. 'You've got
this!' Neill shouted to him as he made the long walk
from the halfway line to the penalty area. So many of
Harry's friends and family were there at Wembley to
watch him win. He couldn't let them down.

Harry placed the ball down on the spot and took a
few steps backwards. He looked down at the ball and
then up at the target. 'You've got this!' he told himself

as he started his run-up. The keeper dived to his left and Harry smashed his shot straight down the middle.

Goooooooooooooooooooaaaaaaaaaaaaaaaalllllllllllll llllllllllllll!!!!!!!!!!!!!!!!!!!!

Harry didn't show any emotion. He just picked the ball out of the net, put it back on the spot, and walked back to his teammates.

The penalty shoot-out went all the way to the eleventh men. It was goalkeeper vs goalkeeper! Smithies went first... and scored.

It was all down to Simonsen now. He stepped up... and blasted the ball over the bar!

Sheffield United would not be playing in the Championship next season. As the Huddersfield players celebrated, Harry stood there, frozen in a daze of despair. It was the most painful moment he had ever experienced. That horrible sinking feeling was nothing compared to this.

'Head up, kid,' Wilson said as he walked over to give Harry a reassuring hug. 'You should be so proud of what you've achieved this season. Unbelievable! You'll be back – *we'll* be back.'

CHAPTER 11

GAME AFTER GAME

After Harry's fantastic breakthrough season in 2011–12, lots of clubs wanted to sign him. The list even included Premier League teams like Newcastle United. Was it time to move on to bigger things?

A few Sheffield United players did move on. Right-back Matthew Lowton joined Aston Villa, and midfielder Stephen Quinn joined Hull City. Harry, however, chose to stay at the club.

'I don't want to go somewhere else and sit on the bench,' he decided. 'I want to keep playing game after game!'

Week in week out, Harry was the star of the Blades' defence. He was already the Bramall Lane hero that he had hoped to be. During the 2011–12 season, he had played in fifty-six matches. That was a massive number for a teenager!

'At a Premier League club, I might not even play ten proper matches,' Harry argued. 'No thanks!'

First-team experience was so important, no matter which division it was in. Harry needed to be playing under pressure, in matches that really mattered. How else was he going to learn and improve as a centre-back? With Neill by his side, Harry was getting a great football education at Sheffield United.

'If you can defend well in League One, you can defend well in the Premier League,' his manager Danny Wilson assured him. 'Trust me, you've got what it takes!'

Plus, Harry couldn't walk away from his local club without having another go at achieving his number one aim – promotion to the Championship.

In the 2012–13 season, Harry's consistency continued. He wore the Number 5 shirt now and he only missed two of United's forty-six league matches.

Game after game, he battled bravely against big, strong strikers.

'No-one's getting past Maguire today!'

Game after game, he used his body to block powerful shots.

'That's heroic defending there from Maguire!'

Game after game, he jumped highest to win headers.

'A towering leap from Maguire!'

Game after game, he stopped goals with his crunching, sliding tackles.

'Maguire with a crucial challenge!'

Game after game, he brought the ball forward out of defence to set up attacks.

'What a run this is from Maguire. Will he go all the way?'

Not only was Harry becoming a brilliant centre-back, but he was also a local lad. The Sheffield United fans loved him even more for that.

Harry, Harry Harry, Harry, Harry, Harry Harry, HARRY MAGUIRE!!

One day, they knew, he would move on to bigger and better things, but they wanted to keep him for as long as possible.

Don't leave us, Harry, we love you!

In February 2013, he made his 100th senior start for Sheffield United, and he was still not quite twenty years old. He felt like an experienced professional now, even if he didn't look like one.

'Sometimes, I forget how young you are,' Neill joked, 'but then I look at your awful clothes and your scruffy haircut, and I remember!'

What did Harry wish for on his twentieth birthday? Promotion to the Championship, of course.

'Come on, we can do it!' he told his teammates.

Again, Sheffield United were in the top six all season but again, they finished in the play-off places. Last year's Wembley defeat to Huddersfield still haunted them but Harry stayed positive. He was desperate to play at a higher level.

'This is our year, lads!'

The Blades beat Yeovil Town 1–0 in the first leg at Bramall Lane and the team travelled to Huish Park feeling confident. The sun was shining and United were wearing their black and red away kit, the colours of Harry's childhood club, Brunsmeer Athletic. It was going to be a good day.

In the first few minutes, however, Yeovil scored. It was now 1–1 on aggregate. Harry kicked the air in frustration. What a terrible start!

Sheffield United didn't give up, though. They fought back and nearly grabbed the goal they needed. Jamie Murphy's curling shot crashed against the crossbar. So close!

'Unlucky, keep going!' Harry called out.

In the last few minutes, Yeovil crossed a hopeful ball into the box. It flew over Harry's head and fell to their striker, Ed Upson. Harry watched in horror as Upson's header whizzed towards the top corner.

No, no, NO! Harry turned away in disgust. He couldn't bear to see the ball land in the back of the net. There would be no return trip to Wembley Stadium. Their season was over.

Nothing could ease Harry's pain – not even another Sheffield United Player of the Year award, and not even a spot in the League One Team of the Year for the second year in a row.

Yes, he was Mr Consistent, but would Harry ever be able to lift his team out of the lower leagues?

CHAPTER 12

ENGLAND CALLING – PART ONE

The older Harry got, the more he thought back to his childhood dreams. He had achieved so many of them already. He was a professional footballer, and a very successful one too. He was playing for his favourite club, Sheffield United, and the fans loved him. He had scored goals at Bramall Lane and he had even played at Wembley. What else was left?

International football! Ever since World Cup 2002, Harry had been England's biggest fan. For the most important matches, the Maguire family liked to throw massive parties at their house. Wearing his white England shirt, Harry watched and hoped.

His heroes were the two centre-backs: Rio

Ferdinand and John Terry. They were the best in the business – calm, quick, strong, and classy on the ball.

'With those guys at the back, we can't lose!' Harry thought, but sadly, he thought wrong.

He was miserable when England lost on penalties to Portugal at Euro 2004.

'We were robbed!'

He was devastated when the same thing happened again at the 2006 World Cup.

'How could Cristiano Ronaldo get Wayne Rooney sent off like that? They play together at Manchester United!'

He was heartbroken when England didn't even qualify for Euro 2008.

'Who am I going to support now?'

England fared a little better in the 2010 World Cup but Harry was still disappointed when they got thrashed by their old rivals Germany. Then at Euro 2012, they lost on penalties… AGAIN!

'We're cursed!' Harry told his best friend, Danny.

For years, Harry only thought about supporting England – on TV and at Wembley. The idea of actually *playing* for England seemed impossible!

Once he became a Sheffield United's best centre-back, however, people started talking about a call-up to the Under-21s. He didn't want to get his hopes up, though.

'They hardly ever give League One players a chance,' he reminded his brothers.

In November 2012, that all changed. The England Under-21s were about to play a friendly match against Northern Ireland but they were struggling for numbers. Jason Lowe and Sammy Ameobi were both injured and Wilfried Zaha had been called up to the senior squad.

'Is it too late to call up a few extras?' the Under-21s manager Stuart Pearce asked his coaches.

No, it wasn't, because the match was nearby – at Blackpool's Bloomfield Road stadium. The first player they asked was Leicester City striker Martyn Waghorn. And the second? Harry, of course!

At first, he didn't believe it. Was it Danny playing a prank on him? No, it really was Stuart Pearce on the phone, calling him up to the England Under-21s.

'Wow, thanks, it's a real honour!' Harry replied, trying not to sound too much like a star-struck kid.

But that was exactly how he felt at first. He was the only League One player in the squad and many of his new teammates were already Premier League stars. Harry watched them on *Match of the Day* every Saturday night.

Connor Wickham played for Sunderland, Andros Townsend played for Tottenham, and Nick Powell played for Manchester United. Captain Jordan Henderson had signed for Liverpool for nearly £20million!

'Welcome to the team!' Jordan said with a smile.

Harry had no idea if he would get to play in the match but it was a great experience to train with such brilliant players and coaches. Was he good enough to compete at this level? Of course, he was. He just had to believe in himself.

'Blimey, you're a beast!' Connor told him after receiving one of his trademark tackles.

At Bloomfield Road, Harry watched the first half from the subs bench. The England Under-21s had

won all of their matches in 2012 and Northern
Ireland were no match for them. Harry was
impressed by his team's flowing, passing football. He
couldn't wait to join in if he got the opportunity…

Jordan and Josh McEachran created chance after
chance and eventually, Connor headed home. 1–0!

England were winning but Pearce wanted more.
After sixty minutes, he made a triple substitution.
Benik Afobe came on for Andros in attack, Nathaniel
Clyne came on for Adam Smith at right-back, and
Harry came on for Andre Wisdom at centre-back.

Wearing the white Number 15 shirt, Harry jogged
out onto the pitch. The 9,000 supporters in the
stadium clapped quietly. It was a cold Tuesday night
in Blackpool, rather than a sell-out at Wembley, but
Harry didn't care about that. He was an England
international now! The last of his childhood dreams
was coming true.

'Right, focus!' Harry told himself.

He could enjoy his proud moment with his family.
For now, he had some defending to do. If he played
well, maybe Pearce would call him up again.

The last thirty minutes flew by in a flash. What could Harry do to leave his mark on the match? He did his best to show off his heading and his passing, as the Three Lions cruised to victory. There were no goals or heroic blocks, but he was pleased with his debut, and so was his manager.

'Well done, you looked really comfortable out there!' Pearce said at the final whistle, shaking his hand.

Harry was still buzzing when he returned to Sheffield United.

'Oh, here comes our England star,' his teammates teased. 'We better roll out the red carpet!'

Harry laughed along but that taste of international football had made him more focused than ever. Now, he knew that he could do it – he was good enough to reach the highest level. With hard work and determination, he could one day play in the Premier League, and perhaps even play for his country at a major tournament.

Although that turned out to be Harry's one and only appearance for the Under-21s, his England days were far from over.

CHAPTER 13

GOAL MACHINE!

Neill and the new Sheffield United manager Chris Morgan were always reminding Harry about the rules of being a centre-back:

'Defend first, and attack second.'

'If in doubt, get it out!'

'Safety first!'

Harry knew the rules but every now and then, he couldn't help breaking them.

'If I see space ahead of me, why shouldn't I dribble forward?' he thought. That was his old mid-fielder brain talking. Sometimes it was a little risky but most of the time, it really helped the team to attack.

Harry could weave his way through tackles, he

could play perfect long passes, and he could score goals too.

In the Football League Trophy second round against Notts County in October 2012, Harry chased after a clearance. From way out on the right wing, he calmly curled the ball over the goalkeeper's outstretched arm and in off the post.

Goooooooooooooaaaaaaaaalllllllllllllllllllllll!!!!!!!!!!!!

'Extraordinary!' the TV commentator cried out, as Harry celebrated with his teammates.

'Was it a shot, or was it a cross?' they asked.

'Of course it was a shot!' he told them confidently.

If Ronaldinho could claim that goal against England in the 2002 World Cup, then Harry was definitely claiming this one.

During the 2012–13 League One season, he scored once with his right foot and twice with his powerful head.

'That nearly burst the net!' his teammate Nick Blackman cheered, giving him a big high-five.

As a defender, Harry loved keeping clean sheets and making important tackles, but scoring goals was also really fun. It was an amazing feeling to hear the fans at Bramall Lane cheering his name.

Harry, Harry Harry, Harry, Harry, Harry Harry, HARRY MAGUIRE!!

Harry was always looking for ways to improve – more tackles, more passes, more dribbles, and more goals.

On the first day of the 2013–14 season, Sheffield United were once again playing Notts County, this time at home. They were drawing 1–1, but that really wasn't the result that the Blades wanted – they wanted to win!

Stephen McGinn curled a free-kick all the way to Harry at the back post. He watched the ball carefully as it dropped down towards him. He was unmarked, but it was going to take a brilliant header to beat the keeper from there. BOOM! Like a bullet, the ball flew into the top corner of the net.

Goooooooooooooaaaaaaaaaallllllllllllllllllllllllll!!!!!!!!!!!!

Harry ran over to the Sheffield United fans with his arms in the air and a massive smile on his face. It was the winning goal and he was the hero.

Two weeks later, the Blades were losing 1–0 to Colchester United. Febian Brandy passed a quick free kick to Harry near the halfway line.

'Shoot! Shoot!' the fans urged.

Why not? Harry dribbled forward and hit a swerving, long-range right foot rocket. It wasn't his best strike ever but it caught the goalkeeper by surprise. He spilled the ball into his own net!

Goooooooooooooaaaaaaaaaalllllllllllllllllllllll!!!!!!!!!!!!

Harry pointed up at his family in the stands and punched the air. Two goals in three games – what a start to the season!

'What would we do without you?' his manager asked.

Two months later, Harry was still Sheffield United's joint top scorer with two goals. The Blades were bottom of the league. What a disaster! They needed a hero more than ever.

Against Crewe Alexandra, a cross bounced across the penalty area, and Harry reacted quicker than any of the defenders around him. With a clever header, he steered the ball low into the bottom corner. 1–0!

'Get in!' Harry roared but he wasn't done yet. Ten minutes later, he scored another header to make it 2–0.

Goooooooooooooaaaaaaaaaallllllllllllllllllllllllll!!!!!!!!!!!!

Harry was definitely his team's top scorer now! Those goals gave Sheffield United the confidence to climb back up the table. By the end of 2013, they were out of the relegation zone but Harry was still their top scorer.

'Maybe I should play up front instead!' he joked.

From corners and free kicks, Harry was simply unstoppable in the air.

Step One: He used his strength to outmuscle his marker.

Step Two: He used his height to win the header. *BOOM!*

Step Three: He used his power and technique to find the back of the net. *GOAL!*

Eventually, Chris Porter took over as United's top scorer, but Harry only finished two goals behind him. He was becoming an amazing all-round player – defender *and* attacker.

CHAPTER 14

BATTLING WITH THE BIG BOYS

Sheffield United didn't quite make it to the League One play-offs in 2014, but the season was still a big success.

The Blades hadn't got past the fifth round of the FA Cup in years but suddenly, they were beating everybody: Colchester United, Cambridge United... even Aston Villa!

Against Villa, it was Harry vs Christian Benteke, their big Belgian target man. Some young players would have been nervous but Harry couldn't wait to test himself against one of the Premier League's strongest strikers.

'Let the battle begin!' Harry told Neill.

Wherever Benteke went, Harry was always right behind him. He was a big centre-back but he was also quick and clever, and the Belgian couldn't escape from him.

With every header and block, Harry grew in confidence. He felt ten feet tall! He couldn't get carried away, though. This was top-level football. Everything could change in a second. Harry had to stay focused until the final whistle.

FWEEEEEEEEEEEEEET!

It was over – Aston Villa 1 Sheffield United 2. The players ran around hugging each other as if they had just won the FA Cup. It was a proud day that Harry would never forget. He had won his biggest battle yet!

'See, you're Premier League quality, big man!' Neill told him, feeling like a proud parent.

Could the Blades pull off another cup upset against Fulham? Yes!

Harry got the ball near the halfway line and dribbled forward at speed.

'Keep going!' the Bramall Lane crowd screamed. They were up on their feet, waiting, hoping...

On the edge of the penalty area, Harry shrugged off a tackle and crossed the ball to Chris. 1–0 to Sheffield United!

Harry punched the air. He was helping his team at both ends of the pitch.

When their captain, Michael Doyle got sent off, it was Harry who took the armband. He was still only twenty years old but he was a born leader.

'Stay strong, we can do this!' he called out to his nine teammates. He was always talking, always organising the defence.

In the seventy-fifth minute, Fulham's Hugo Rodallega got the ball on the edge of the box. Harry threw himself to the floor to try and block the shot but it flew past him and into the bottom corner. 1–1!

'No!' Harry lay on the grass with his head in his hands for a few seconds, but then he got back up and carried on. He had to. Sheffield United needed to hold on for a draw and a replay.

At Craven Cottage, United won a corner in the very last minute. This was their last chance to score, before the match went to penalties.

Harry stood near the back post, waving his arms in the air. 'On my head!' he called out to Jose Baxter. The cross was brilliant and so was Harry's header back across goal to Shaun Miller. 2–1 – they were through to the FA Cup Fifth Round!

Again, the players celebrated like they had just won the whole competition. It was such an exciting time to be a Sheffield United player or supporter. Harry was both, so it was doubly exciting for him.

'United! United!' he cheered.

The Blades were on a roll. They beat Nottingham Forest 3–1 and then Charlton Athletic 2–0 to make it through to the FA Cup semi-finals. It was a fantastic achievement for a team in League One.

'Wembley, here we come!' Harry yelled at the top of his voice. He couldn't wait to return to the Home of Football, and win this time.

The fans couldn't wait either. Thousands of them travelled down to London for the game against Hull City. One more win and Sheffield United would be in the final for the first time since 1936.

At half-time, they were 2–1 up and halfway there.

'Just keep going lads,' their manager encouraged them. 'You're all heroes already but if we win this, you'll be legends!'

In the second half, however, Hull fought back with two quick goals. There was nothing that Harry could do to stop them. Sheffield United were in shock and they fell apart. It was game over, and the end of their incredible cup run.

'What a nightmare!' Harry muttered to himself at the final whistle. In his head, he kept replaying all five of Hull's goals. 'We let in FIVE - what was I doing out there today?'

'Don't be so hard on yourself, you played well,' Neill said, putting an arm around his shoulder. 'Without you, there's no way we would have got this far. No way!'

Once his disappointment faded, Harry looked back happily on his FA Cup adventure. He was particularly proud of his performances against the Premier League clubs, Aston Villa and Fulham. He had battled against the big boys, and won both times. Harry now felt ready to do that week in week out, game after game.

CHAPTER 15

HEADING FOR HULL

By the end of the 2013–14 season, Harry was one
of the highest-rated youngsters in English football. If
scouts hadn't already known about him, they certainly
did after Sheffield United's incredible cup run.

'He's got great feet for a big centre-back!'

'Look at that composure on the ball – he can
really play!'

Scouts from Manchester United, Chelsea and
Tottenham came and went. Arsenal sent their old
defender Martin Keown to Bramall Lane.

'Maguire's very good,' Keown reported back,
'but I'm not sure he's quick enough for the Premier
League.'

It was Championship club Wolves who made the first bid of £1 million for Harry.

'No way!' Sheffield United said firmly.

Wolves came back with a second bid: £1.5 million.

'No way!' Sheffield United said firmly again. 'Harry's worth a lot more than that.'

Soon, they received a higher bid from Hull City. Harry couldn't believe it. 'They still want to buy me after the FA Cup semi-final?'

Yes! The Tigers had been watching Harry for years in League One. Eventually, their main scout, Stan Ternent, decided to speak to the manager, Steve Bruce.

'There's a young defender at Sheffield United that I think you should take a look at.'

'Okay, what's his name?'

'Harry Maguire. He's only twenty-one but he's already played 150 games for them! He's tall, he's strong, and he's talented with the ball too. He's been in the League One Team of the Year for the last two years. I think he's ready for the next step but see what you think.'

'Thanks for the recommendation, Stan. I'll go and watch him play.'

Bruce was very impressed by Harry's stats but what about his actual skills? The Hull manager was very impressed by those as well.

At first, he just looked like another big, beefy centre-back, who wrestled with strikers and won lots of headers.

'No, we won't need one of those in the Premier League,' Bruce muttered to himself.

But then Harry got the ball down and started to play. He passed and moved up the pitch, turning defence into attack. He had the confidence to take players on and dribble straight past them.

'Wow!' The Hull manager was blown away by Harry's composure. '*That* is exactly what we need in the Premier League!'

When the Tigers played Sheffield United in the FA Cup semi-final in April 2014, Bruce got another chance to see Harry in action. Harry didn't have his best game in defence but he still created lots of chances in attack when he brought the ball forward. The Hull midfielders couldn't cope with his confident, powerful runs.

'He looks like he's been playing at this level for years,' Bruce told his assistant, Steve Agnew. 'We *have* to sign him, before someone else does!'

Sheffield United rejected Hull's first offer of £2 million but the second was too good to turn down: £2.5 million was a lot of money for a League One club.

'We really want you to stay here,' the Blades manager, Nigel Clough, told his star player, 'but it's your choice now. Have a think about it.'

The more Harry thought about it, the more excited he became. If he signed for Hull City, he would finally get to play in the Premier League, and the Europa League too! That had been his dream for years. He would get to play alongside experienced stars like Curtis Davies, Michael Dawson and Tom Huddlestone. Harry knew that he could learn so much from Hull's players, and also from Hull's manager.

Bruce had been a brilliant centre-back for

Manchester United in the 1990s, winning three
Premier League titles alongside legends like Ryan
Giggs, David Beckham and Eric Cantona. Harry was
sure that he would have lots of great advice for a
young defender with big ambition.

'It's time for a new challenge,' he told his parents.
'I'm ready!'

'Of course you are,' they reassured him. 'We
believe in you!'

It would be sad to say goodbye to Sheffield United
after so many happy years, but what if Harry never
got another opportunity like this? If he didn't take it,
he might regret it forever.

It also helped that Hull was only an hour's drive
away from Sheffield. Harry wasn't yet ready to leave
his family, and Yorkshire, behind.

'I'm sorry but I can't stay another season,' he told
Clough. 'This is my chance to play in the Premier
League.'

His manager understood. 'Good luck, you're going
to be great!'

After passing the medical and signing the contract,

it was photo time. Harry was a Hull player now!
He stood in the stands of the KC Stadium, wearing
the orange-and-black-striped shirt and holding up an
orange-and-black-striped scarf. There was a big smile
stretched across his face.

'I can't wait to get started!' Harry told the club's
website.

At least he wasn't starting his scary new adventure
alone. On the very same day, Hull also signed a
Scottish left-back. His name was Andrew Robertson
and they quickly became good friends.

'Dundee United? Never heard of them!' Harry
liked to tease Andrew about his former club. 'I
thought there was only one decent team these days –
Celtic.'

'Hey, the Scottish Premier League is still a lot
better than English League One, Big Man!'

Harry was a year older than Andrew but they got
on really well. They were both young players who
had just made the big move to the best league in the
world. Together, they coped with the challenges of
being the new kids at the club. Before the opening

match of the season, they each had to sing a song in front of the entire Hull squad. Andrew went first.

'Excellent, Andy!' the audience cheered and sang along.

'Right, your turn, H!'

Harry was as calm as ever as he stood up on a chair in the middle of the dressing room. The pressure was on. It was time to get the party started:

'Come on, let's twist again!' he sang, shaking his hips from side to side.

The other players were soon rolling on the floor with laughter. What a performance! Somehow, Harry managed to keep his balance and not fall off the chair. When he finished, he got a standing ovation.

'With moves like that, you're going to be a big hit here at Hull!' Curtis predicted.

CHAPTER 16

SLOW START AT HULL

Harry played for Hull in the Europa League and the League Cup, but he had to wait a long time for his Premier League debut. Often, he wasn't even on the bench.

'I don't get it. What am I doing wrong?' Harry asked his family.

'Just keep working hard and be patient,' they replied.

Harry wasn't used to being patient. He wanted to keep playing game after game, just like he had at Sheffield United. The Hull coaches, however, didn't think he was ready for that.

'We need to get you fitter first,' they told him.

That was one of the biggest differences between League One and the Premier League. In order to compete against teams like Chelsea and Manchester City, Harry needed to be a lean, mean running machine! Otherwise, strikers like Diego Costa and Sergio Agüero would destroy him again and again.

'They'll turn you inside out if you're not careful!' Curtis and Michael warned him.

Harry was a big, strong centre-back but he needed to be agile too. In the top division, teams attacked with so much skill and speed. How would he cope with that? It was time for Harry to get serious about his lifestyle. He needed to start eating better and sleeping better.

'I'll do anything to play in the Premier League!' he told his coaches at Hull.

With that positive, can-do attitude, Harry got fitter and fitter. Andrew was playing week in week out at left wing-back, and that spurred him on. Soon, that would be him! Curtis and Michael were playing brilliantly, and so was James Chester. Harry was the fourth-choice centre-back but at some point, he would get his chance to shine.

In the meantime, he kept smiling and joined in with all the dressing room jokes. Many of them were about the size of Harry's head.

'Is it hard to find hats that fit?' Tom teased.

He always had a comeback ready. 'Is it hard to find clothes that awful?'

In December 2014, Harry's big moment finally arrived. With fifteen minutes to go against Swansea City, Hull were losing 1–0 and Curtis was injured. Bruce looked at his bench and decided to give Harry an early Christmas present.

'Get forward as much as you can!' the manager told him.

Sure thing! Harry ran onto the pitch, proudly wearing the Number 12 shirt. He could now call himself a Premier League player.

'Go on, Big Man!' Andrew called to him.

Harry was desperate to become Hull's new hero. This was it – his chance to shine. Unfortunately, there was no time for him to attack. Instead, Harry had defending to do. He batted bravely in the air against Wilfried Bony and Marvin Emnes.

Before Harry knew it, the match was over. His Premier League debut had ended in defeat. Hull were now deep in the relegation zone. If only he could help...

But no, Harry was back on the bench in the Hull games against Sunderland and Leicester City. Had that been his one and only chance?

Against Everton, Harry came on with thirty minutes to go. Hull were winning 2–0.

'Just keep things tight,' Bruce told him.

Sure thing! Harry stayed focused until the final whistle. There was no way he was going to let Romelu Lukaku or Arouna Koné score.

'Well played, H!' Curtis cheered as they celebrated a very important victory.

Was this Harry's big breakthrough? He hoped so but no, he was back on the bench again for the next game.

Against West Ham, Harry came on at half-time. The score was still 0–0 – what a chance for him to shine! He couldn't wait to play a whole forty-five minutes of football.

Oh dear! Thirty minutes later, Hull were losing badly. When Alex Song played a defence-splitting pass, Harry couldn't keep up with Stewart Downing. 3–0! That horrible sinking feeling was back.

'I just need more game-time!' he groaned.

The only answer was to go out on loan. Harry joined Wigan Athletic and stayed until the end of the season. It felt weird wearing blue and white, like United's Sheffield rivals, Wednesday, but he was willing to do anything for game-time.

Playing in the Championship, Harry's confidence came back quickly. In his first game against Reading, in February 2015, Wigan kept a cleansheet and won for the first time in months.

'Thank goodness you're here!' his new manager Malky Mackay said.

Harry was just happy to be playing game after game again. He was Mr Consistent at the heart of the Wigan defence, winning headers and crunching tackles.

And he got forward to attack too. Away at Blackpool, a corner-kick came in and he won the header at the back post.

Goooooooooooooooooooaaaaaaaaaaaaaaaaaalllllllllllll lllllllllllllll!!!!!!!!!!!!!!!!!!!!!

The old Harry was back! He ran over to the fans, shaking his fists in the air. 'Get in!' he roared, with joy rushing through his veins.

Harry did his best to rescue Wigan from relegation. He really didn't want to go back down to League One again. Unfortunately, his efforts were too little, too late.

'I've played every game since I've been here, and I've enjoyed my time here,' Harry told the local newspapers. 'The lads and the staff have been brilliant, it's a great club.'

He was sad to leave Wigan in such a bad state but things weren't much better back at Hull either. They had just been relegated from the Premier League to the Championship.

'Wherever I go, I bring bad luck!' Harry told his brothers, and he was only half-joking.

The news wasn't all negative, though. During the summer of 2015, James Chester joined West Brom for £8 million. When Bristol City then tried to sign Harry, Bruce said no.

Hopefully, that meant that Harry would now get lots more game-time at Hull. After a slow start, it was time for Sheffield's star to shine.

CHAPTER 17

PROMOTION AT LAST!

Again, however, Harry had to be patient. Michael and Curtis started the Championship season as Hull's first-choice centre-backs.

'Don't worry, your time will come,' Bruce promised.

But when? Sometimes, Harry forgot that he was still only twenty-two. While he waited, he tried to learn as much as he could from his experienced teammates. Michael and Curtis were always happy to help whenever he had any questions.

'Communication is key,' Michael told him. 'I know I talk a lot out on the pitch but that's a big part of my job! It keeps the defence alert and organised.'

Of course, Harry really didn't want either of his

teammates to get injured, but how else was he going to get into the team? He was desperate to get back to playing game after game.

'Maybe one of them will get a red card instead!' his mum suggested.

Sometimes, Andrew kept Harry company on the Hull bench. It was nice to have supportive friends by his side.

'One day, we'll be Premier League stars and we'll look back on these bad days and laugh. Trust me!'

Slowly but surely, Harry fought his way into the team. First, he played ten minutes, then twenty, then seventy against Brentford. In a back three with Michael and Curtis, he had the freedom to attack, as well as defend.

'Up you go, Big Man!' Curtis called out whenever Hull won a corner-kick.

Harry was causing all kinds of trouble in the Brentford penalty area. He headed the ball into the danger zone and when it bounced back to him, he pulled his right leg back and BANG! The goalkeeper saved his shot but Sam Clucas was there for the rebound. 2–0! Harry and Sam celebrated by sliding across the grass on their knees.

'Premier League, here we come!' they cheered together.

The Tigers were top of the table and full of confidence. How could Bruce put Harry back on the bench after that? He couldn't!

Harry played instead of Curtis, and Hull beat their promotion rivals Middlesbrough 3–0. It was the best team performance of the season.

'Keep up the good work!' his manager told Harry with a big thumbs-up.

Harry played instead of Michael, and Hull beat Reading 2–1. The more games he played, the better he became. Sometimes, Harry took a few risks but he worked and worked to help his team to win. The fans loved his all-action style.

Against QPR, he beat two opponents to the ball and sent them both flying!

'That's it, Harry!'

Against Cardiff, he went up for a corner and a defender wrestled him to the floor. Penalty!

'They just can't handle him!'

Hull were on a roll. Their deadly defence kept cleansheets against Cardiff City, Charlton Athletic, Fulham, Blackburn Rovers… The list went on and on.

'I told you everything would work out for us!' Andrew reminded Harry.

But just when he was feeling on top of the world, Michael returned from injury – and Harry was back on the bench again.

'But I was playing really well!' he moaned.

It seemed so cruel to just drop him like that. Without Harry, Hull slipped from first place down to fourth.

'Bring back Maguire!' the supporters cried out.

Harry came back with a bang against Brentford. In the thirtieth minute, the Hull goalkeeper rolled the ball out to him in defence. After a few sideways passes, Harry saw the space ahead of him and galloped forward.

As usual, Andrew was making a brilliant run down the left wing. Harry spotted it and his long, diagonal ball was an absolute beauty. It floated just over the right-back's head and dropped down in front of Andrew. His cross was so dangerous that the Brentford centre-back could only kick it into his own net. 1–0!

'Keep Maguire in the team!' the supporters cried out.

Sadly, it was too late for Hull to win the Championship title now. The Tigers would have to win promotion through the play-offs instead.

'Not again!' Harry thought to himself.

Twice, he had got to the League One Play-offs with Sheffield United and twice, they had lost. Was it bad luck or bad mistakes? Harry had been relegated twice, and how many times had he been promoted? Zero!

In the play-offs, Bruce selected Michael and Curtis at the back, and Harry on the bench. Hull beat Derby County 3–2 to reach the final at Wembley.

'Well done, lads!' Harry cheered. Even though he wasn't playing in the team, he was still a great team player. 'We're nearly there!'

The final was one of the tightest and nerviest matches that Harry had ever seen. After all, Hull and Sheffield Wednesday were battling each other for a place in the Premier League. What a prize for the winner!

On the bench, Harry looked up at the 70,000 fans and listened to their non-stop noise. How he wished that he could be out there, playing on the pitch against United's Sheffield rivals. Hull needed a hero...

That hero turned out to be midfielder Mohamed Diamé. With twenty minutes to go, he hit a thirty-yard screamer into the top corner. 1–0!

At that moment, Harry was warming up along the touchline. He stopped to watch the ball fly past the goalkeeper and then raced over to join the big team hug.

'Mo, what a beauty!' he yelled.

In the end, Harry did get to play a part in Hull's big day at Wembley. With five minutes to go, he came on to replace Mohamed. The manager's instructions were simple:

'Just don't let them score!'

Those five minutes were the longest of Harry's life. Wednesday had shot after shot but Hull held on.

'Yes, yes, YES!' Harry screamed at the final whistle. 'We're back in the Premier League!'

He had won promotion at last. Harry was the third player up the stadium steps to shake hands and collect his winners' medal. Once it was placed around his neck, suddenly it all felt real. He turned to his captain, Michael, and grabbed him by the face.

'We did it, Daws!' he grinned. 'We did it!'

The players were bouncing up and down before Michael even lifted the trophy. He passed the big silver cup down the line until, eventually, Harry had it in his hands. He kissed the trophy twice and lifted it above his head. What a feeling, in front of all his friends and family at Wembley!

Back down on the pitch, the Hull players posed for team photos together. Harry was right at the centre, dancing, smiling, and shielding his eyes from the spraying champagne.

'Curtis, stop aiming for me!'

'Sorry, your big head's an easy target!'

The celebrations carried on all afternoon and all night too. Harry couldn't wait to be back in the Premier League. This time, he was going to prove himself at the highest level.

CHAPTER 18

AGAINST THE ODDS

As the 2016–17 Premier League season kicked-off, fans disagreed about which team would finish top:

'I reckon Tottenham can do it. They came so close last season and they've got more experience this time around.'

'No, it's going to be Manchester City's year. They've got Pep Guardiola in charge now, and the guy's a genius!'

'What about José Mourinho at Manchester United? He sure knows how to win the Premier League!'

At the other end of the table, most fans agreed about which team would finish bottom:

'Hull City.'

'Yeah, they're going to get hammered every week!'

'They could be relegated by Christmas!'

It had been a very hard summer for Hull. First, their right-back Moses Odubajo picked up a really bad injury in preseason. Then, their manager Steve Bruce resigned and their captain Michael hurt his knee. Finally, their play-off hero Mohamed signed for Newcastle United. Bit by bit, the club's Premier League excitement was fading away.

'Oh no, this is going to be a disaster!' the Hull fans feared.

The opening game against Leicester City was only weeks away, and the Tigers still only had twelve fit players in their first-team squad.

'Come on, lads, we've got to stick together here!' their new manager, Mike Phelan, told them.

Thankfully, there was a strong team spirit amongst the players. They didn't mind battling against the odds.

Harry certainly wasn't giving up on his Premier League dream. He had spent the summer working really hard on every aspect of his game.

On the training pitch, he focused on his fitness. Thanks to the new sports technology, he could look at lots of running stats every day: distance, average speed, and number of sprints. He challenged himself to get faster and faster.

'Look at that acceleration!' Andrew joked. 'Agüero better watch out!'

Off the training pitch, Harry sat through hours and hours of his own performances on video. He found it really embarrassing to watch, but it was a great way to learn from his mistakes.

'No! What were you doing there?' he shouted at himself on the screen. 'Concentrate!'

Harry preferred watching videos of other defenders in action. Premier League legends like John Terry and Rio Ferdinand hardly ever made wrong decisions. They read the game so well that they saw the danger coming and dealt with it every time. They made it look so simple.

'One day, I'll reach that level,' Harry told himself.

Sometimes, Phelan watched videos with him and gave him extra advice. He had been Sir Alex

Ferguson's assistant at Manchester United and so he had worked closely with Ferdinand. Harry eagerly asked him question after question.

'What do you think Rio would have done there?'

'How did Rio know that the striker was going to do that?'

'Who do you think Rio preferred playing against – Fernando Torres or Didier Drogba?'

Each answer added to Harry's football education. He had to learn from the best in order to compete with the best.

Harry played the last ten minutes against Manchester United and then the last forty-five minutes against Arsenal and Liverpool. Hull lost all three matches but he didn't let that get him down. It was all good experience. By the time Phelan gave Harry his first-ever Premier League start against Bournemouth, he felt 100 per cent ready.

'Let's do this!' Harry cheered, high-fiving Curtis, his centre-back partner.

Unfortunately, those high hopes only lasted five minutes. Junior Stanislas' free kick hit the post and

Charlie Daniels scored the rebound, despite Harry's brave dive to stop it. 1–0! After that, Hull just collapsed.

Steve Cook jumped highest to win a header against Harry. 2–1!

Robert Snodgrass gave away a penalty. 3–1!

Adam Smith crossed and Stanislas scored. 4–1!

Joshua King's cross landed on Callum Wilson's head. 5–1!

Daniels passed to Dan Gosling and he curled the ball into corner of the net. 6–1!

Hull had been absolutely hammered. As he trudged off the pitch, Harry felt so many negative emotions at once – humiliation, disappointment, guilt, frustration, anger. It was the worst defeat of his entire career. The horrible sinking feeling stayed in his stomach for days.

'What if I never get to play Premier League football again?' he groaned. He was dreading his post-match video session. Phelan had every right to be furious with him for his poor performance.

'Look, that defeat wasn't your fault,' his manager told him. 'We win as a team and we lose as a team. Every player has to take responsibility. The important thing is how you recover. Rio had bad games too but he always bounced straight back. Now, you've got to do the same!'

Phelan was right; Harry was a strong character and it was time to show it.

Ten days later, he was playing for Hull in the FA Cup against Bristol City. In the last minute of the first half, Ryan Mason curled a high corner into the box. Harry timed his run perfectly and headed home at the back-post. 1–0!

Gooooooooooooaaaaaaaaaallllllllllllllllllllllll!!!!!!!!!!!!!

Harry punched the air proudly. He had finally scored his first goal for Hull! Michael ran over and gave him a massive hug.

'Nice one, H!' his captain shouted, patting his big head.

Soon, Harry was playing in the Premier League again too. Against Crystal Palace, he chested the ball down near the halfway line and looked up. Andrew was making a great run down the left but it would take an incredible long pass to reach him. Instead, Harry calmly dribbled past one player and then played it to Hull's striker, Adama Diomande, who turned and scored. 2–2!

'Great work, H!' Michael shouted.

Against Everton, Harry did it again. He collected the ball at the back and bravely brought it forward.

'Keep going!' the fans urged him on.

Why not? Harry had put his Bournemouth disaster behind him. He now felt really comfortable playing Premier League football. It was his time to shine.

The Everton midfielders backed away in fear as Harry galloped through the middle like a race horse. Eventually, one of them tried to stop him. Foul – free kick!

'Brilliant run, H!' Curtis called out.

Robert fired the free-kick straight into the top corner. 2–1 to Hull!

Against the odds, the Tigers were no longer bottom of the table. Harry was loving every minute of his Premier League adventure, despite all the ups and downs.

'It's a good thing I love rollercoaster rides!' he said with a big smile on his face.

CHAPTER 19

ATTACK FROM THE BACK

Unfortunately, the chaos continued. In January 2017, Hull sacked Mike Phelan and replaced him with a young Portuguese manager called Marco Silva.

'I know we don't have a lot of time,' he admitted in his first interview, 'but I want the fans to believe, like I believe.'

Could the Tigers really stay up? It was going to take a miracle, especially when the club sold two of their best players, Jake Livermore and Robert Snodgrass.

'Come on, lads, we've got to stick together here!' Harry told his teammates.

He didn't know much about Silva but they got

on really well straight away. The new manager had big plans for the defence, and for Harry in particular.

'I want you to be the one who brings the ball forward,' Silva told him. 'We're going to attack from the back!'

'No problem!' Harry thought to himself. It was the role that he was born to play.

Silva's first game was the rematch against Bournemouth. Harry had been looking forward to it for months. He was desperate to get revenge for that awful 6–1 thrashing in his first Premier League start. the Tigers were a much better team now, and Harry was a much better player.

It didn't look that way, however, when he gave away a penalty with a clumsy tackle. Hull were 1–0 down after only three minutes.

'No, no, NO!' he screamed.

Harry didn't panic and give up, though. 'That's not what Rio would do,' he thought to himself. He had to stay strong and make things right. He pushed his team up the pitch with his clever dribbling and passing, and Hull fought back to win 3–1. Silva was impressed.

'You showed real character today,' he told Harry. 'Keep it up – you've got some big battles ahead of you!'

At Stamford Bridge, Harry fought ferociously against Chelsea's star striker, Diego Costa. Hull lost 2–0 but Harry picked up the man of the match award for his all-action performance. At the back, he made eight tackles, seven clearances and eight interceptions. In attack, he took more shots than any of his teammates.

'Great game,' Cesc Fàbregas said, shaking his hand at the final whistle. 'I love the way you play!'

At Old Trafford, Harry frustrated Manchester United's legendary striker Zlatan Ibrahimović all game long. And when Harry got the ball at the back, he wasn't afraid to take a few risks in attack. He even dribbled past his old FA Youth Cup opponent, Paul Pogba. The fans loved Harry's confidence and character.

Ohhhh, Harry Maguire!

Ohhhh, Harry Maguire!

0–0 – an important point for Hull!

At the KC Stadium, Harry and his new centre-back partner, Andrea Ranocchia, kept out Liverpool's ace attackers Roberto Firmino and Sadio Mané. Then just before half-time, Harry headed a corner towards goal and Alfred N'Diaye bundled it in. 1–0!

'Thanks, H!' Alfred cheered, putting an arm around his broad shoulders.

Silva's coaching was working wonders. The team looked fitter than ever and they were passing the ball around beautifully.

Harry was keeping Hull's survival hopes alive, at both ends of the field. Once the defending was done, he loved to attack from the back. It really helped that Harry had one of the best friends by his side. He was now the left centre-back, with Andrew next to him at left-back. Together, they formed a perfect partnership – strength *and* speed, great passes *and* great crosses.

With eight games to go, Hull were just one point away from safety.

'Come on lads, we can do this!' Harry kept telling his teammates.

Now that Michael and Curtis weren't playing so often, he was their heroic leader at the back. Wearing the captain's armband, Harry was improving game after game.

At the start of April 2017, Hull faced Middlesbrough in an epic relegation battle. After an awful start, the Tigers really came back roaring.

Lazar Marković poked the ball in after a goalmouth scramble. 1–1!

Abel Hernández set up Oumar Niasse. 2–1!

'That's more like it!' Harry shouted, punching the air with joy and relief.

The game, however, was far from over. There were still sixty minutes left to play. Could Hull hold on for that long?

No, Harry had a better idea. He got the ball deep in his own half and decided to attack from the back. As he looked up, he saw Sam Clucas making a great run down the right wing. Harry found him with the perfect pass. He curled the ball just past a

Middlesbrough midfielder's outstretched foot, and then in between two defenders. Sam crossed it first-time to Abel. 3–1!

Abel pointed at Sam to thank him for the assist but Sam pointed to his centre-back. 'H, what a ball that was!' he screamed above the deafening crowd.

Middlesbrough scored again just before half-time but luckily, Harry wasn't finished yet. With twenty anxious minutes ahead, Hull won a free kick. Andrew whipped the ball into the box, knowing exactly where his big friend would be: the back post! Harry was unmarked but he still had plenty of work to do. He headed the ball over the goalkeeper's arms and it looped down into the far corner of the net. 4–2 – game over!

Goooooooooooooooooooaaaaaaaaaaaaaaaaalllllllllllllllllllllllllll!!!!!!!!!!!!!!!!!!!!

What a time for Harry to score his first Premier League goal! The Hull fans went wild as he ran over and jumped into Michael's arms.

Ohhhh, Harry Maguire!
Ohhhh, Harry Maguire!

There was no stopping him now. Away at
Southampton a few weeks later, Harry was Hull's
hero yet again.

Sofiane Boufal dribbled into the penalty area, past
two flying challenges, but he couldn't get past Harry.
TACKLE!

Nathan Redmond crossed to Dušan Tadić but he
couldn't score past Harry. *BLOCK!*

0–0 – another important point for Hull!

He was really making a name for himself now.
Every Premier League club wanted a 'Harry Maguire'
at the heart of their defence.

'He has very good skills,' Silva praised his captain.
'It's clear to me that he will have a big career in the
future.'

That future, however, would not be at Hull.
Despite his best efforts, they lost their big battles
against Sunderland and Crystal Palace. The
rollercoaster ride had come to an end. Harry was
relegated for the third time in his career.

This time, however, he was going down with
his big head held high. In his first full season in the

Premier League, Harry had been Hull's hero, captain, and Player of the Year.

After the last home game of the season, he walked slowly around the pitch, clapping to the tearful fans. Harry had given 100 per cent to help his team, and they loved him for that.

Ohhhh, Harry Maguire!

Ohhhh, Harry Maguire!

Harry would always be grateful for their support, especially during his difficult early days on the bench. Wow, he had come a long way since then! What was next for Harry?

CHAPTER 20

LEICESTER CITY

Harry was trying to relax on his family summer holiday in Majorca, but he had a difficult decision to make. As he lay there by the pool, soaking up the sun, he asked himself,

'Who do I want to play for next season?'

After his big breakthrough year with Hull, lots of top clubs were queuing up to sign him: Tottenham, Leicester City, Stoke City, Everton, Newcastle United, Southampton, West Ham... The list went on and on.

When his agent told him, Harry's first thought was, 'Great, I'll get to stay in the Premier League!'

Now, however, he had to pick which team to play for. What a hard choice!

Tottenham were the Premier League runners-up for two years in a row. They had an amazing manager, Mauricio Pochettino, and amazing players like Harry Kane, Christian Eriksen and Dele Alli.

'Plus, you'd be playing Champions League football next season!' Laurence argued.

The only problem was that they already had a deadly defence. Toby Alderweireld and Jan Vertonghen were two of the best centre-backs in the world, and they had Eric Dier as well!

'No, there's no way that I'm going to play week in week out at Spurs,' Harry decided.

No matter what, he wasn't going back to the bench again. He was twenty-four years old now. Wherever he went, he needed guaranteed game-time.

Harry moved on to his next option, 'Okay, well how about Leicester City, then?'

The Foxes were the 2015–16 Premier League Champions and they still had their world-class forwards, Jamie Vardy and Riyad Mahrez. Harry could start the attacks from the back and they would finish them off. Easy!

'They've got some other promising young English players too,' Joe argued. 'Ben Chilwell's good, and Demarai Gray's rapid!'

But, most importantly, what about their defence? Did they have space for a new centre-back? Yes, they had a big, Harry-shaped gap to fill!

Robert Huth and Wes Morgan were both coming towards the end of their careers and Leicester City didn't really have a back-up option.

'Maguire is our man!' their manager, Craig Shakespeare, decided.

He was so desperate to sign Harry that he flew all the way out to Majorca to meet him.

'I hope you're having a nice summer holiday,' Shakespeare began. 'This shouldn't take long. I'm rebuilding the Leicester defence and I want to rebuild it around you!'

That sounded awesome but Harry didn't want to rush into things. This was the biggest decision of his life, and he had to get it right. He had lots of questions for the Leicester manager:

What formation would the team be playing – 4–4–2 or 3–5–2?

What style of football did he want his team to play?

And what were the club's expectations for the season ahead – Top Four, Top Six or Top Ten?

As he answered each question, Shakespeare grew more and more impressed. Harry was clearly a very clever young man, who studied football closely. It only made the Leicester manager even more determined to sign him.

Harry grew more and more impressed too. Not only had Shakespeare come all the way to a Spanish island to speak to him, but he had big, bold plans for the football club.

'And I want you to be a key part of it!' the manager told him passionately.

Leicester were building towards a brighter future. They were improving their academy, their training ground, and, of course, their squad. The Foxes were on the up and they were aiming for European qualification.

'Perfect, where do I sign?' Harry thought to himself.

He didn't want to join a global giant like Manchester United or Chelsea. That wasn't his style. Leicester was a family club that cared about its local community, just like his home team, Sheffield United. He knew that he would be very happy there.

'I've made up my mind,' Harry told his family at dinner one night. 'I'm going to Leicester!'

It was a sad day when Harry went back to say goodbye to all his friends at Hull. They felt like family.

'Good luck, Big H!' Michael cheered.

'Cheers for everything, Daws. I couldn't have done it without you!'

'I'm going to miss playing with you!' Andrew said as they hugged.

'Me too, mate! Why don't you just come with me?'

Back in 2014, Hull had paid £2.5 million to sign Harry from Sheffield United. Three years later, Leicester were writing a much, much larger cheque.

'£17million for someone who just got relegated?' people on Twitter reacted. 'The world's gone crazy!'

'That Hull defence let in eighty goals last season. Leicester are having a laugh!'

Yes, it was an awful lot of money, but there was only one way that Harry could prove his value – by performing well out on the pitch.

First, however, Leicester's new Number 15 needed to settle in. It didn't take him long to make new friends in the squad. There were lots of big, fun characters at the club.

'Alright mate, is it true that you're an Owls fan like me?' Jamie teased. He was from Sheffield too, and had started out in the Wednesday youth team.

Harry rolled his eyes. 'Stop winding me up, you know I'm a Blade through and through!'

Harry quickly became a popular member of the Leicester dressing room, and a key member of the team. He scored his first goal for his new club in August 2017 against Burton Albion and, for once, it wasn't even a header. As the ball bounced down in the box, he smashed it home with his right foot.

Goooooooooooooooooooaaaaaaaaaaaaaaaaalllllllllllll llllllllllllllll!!!!!!!!!!!!!!!!!!!!

It was only a preseason friendly, but Harry meant business. He had new targets for the new year.

'Every player wants to play for their country,' he told the journalists afterwards. 'I felt like this was the club that could help me progress into the England squad.'

Some people laughed at Harry's ambition, but he was being deadly serious. This was going to be *his* season.

With Robert Huth out injured, Harry started alongside Wes Morgan against Arsenal. It wasn't the solid defensive debut that he was hoping for, but he played his part in attack.

In the fifth minute, Harry crept in at the back post, as usual, to head the ball back for Shinji Okazaki. 1–1!

'Thanks, H!' Shinji cheered, giving him a big hug.

A week later against Brighton and Hove Albion, Harry got a cleansheet and a goal. It was a trademark towering header at the back post.

Goooooooooooooooooooaaaaaaaaaaaaaaaalllllllllllll llllllllllllllll!!!!!!!!!!!!!!!!!!!!

As Harry celebrated in front of the fans, Wilfred Ndidi and Wes jumped up on his back. He was so strong that he could carry them both!

'£17million, eh?' Jamie laughed. 'What a bargain for that big head of yours!'

Suddenly, Harry's dreams of a first England call-up didn't seem so silly at all.

CHAPTER 21

ENGLAND CALLING — PART TWO

Even though he was a Premier League star now, Harry was still England's biggest fan. When his brothers and friends went to France to watch Euro 2016, he decided to join them.

'Three Lions on a shirt!' he sang along with the rest of the supporters in Saint-Étienne. As long as he didn't sing too loudly, or badly, he could blend into the crowd.

The match finished Slovakia 0 England 0. It wasn't the most exciting game of football that Harry had ever seen, but the trip was worth it for the amazing atmosphere alone. The fans showed so much passion, even when their team wasn't playing very well.

'You should be out there playing, H!' his brothers told him.

Harry looked down at the white shirt he was wearing, and the blue Three Lions over his heart. Then he looked up at the players on the pitch. Nathaniel Clyne, Jordan Henderson – he had played with both of them for the Under-21s. In that moment, anything seemed possible.

A year later, after a sensational season at Hull and a big-money move to Leicester, Harry's England dream seemed more than possible. The national team manager Gareth Southgate was watching him closely.

'Every kid wants to play for their country,' Harry told the media. 'I want to play in the World Cup.'

Dele Alli, Raheem Sterling, Harry Kane – Harry Maguire was competing against the best players every week in the Premier League. And then there was Jamie, Harry's Leicester teammate.

'If Vards can play for England, then so can I!' he told himself.

In August 2017, nearly five years after his only

cap for the Under-21s, Harry finally got the call-up
he was hoping for. He was named in Southgate's
squad for the World Cup qualifiers against Malta and
Slovakia.

'I did it!' he told his family on the phone. 'I'm in!'

It was yet another proud moment for all the
Maguires.

When Harry joined the squad at St George's Park,
he made a bigger entrance than he had expected.
While the other England players arrived with their
designer clothes and fancy suitcases, he turned up
in his Leicester tracksuit, with his boots and shin
pads in a black bin bag. The photos were trending on
social media in seconds.

'Harry Maguire looks like he's moving into student
halls in freshers' week,' someone wrote on Twitter.

When the news reached Harry's mum, she wasn't
happy.

'A bin bag?' she told him off via text message.
'What were you thinking? So embarrassing!'

'Sorry, Mum!' Harry replied quickly.

'If I get called up again, I'll treat myself to some

proper luggage!' he joked with the journalists.

Out on the training pitch, however, Harry was 100 per cent focused on football. This was his big chance to impress Southgate. In the squad of twenty-eight players, there were at least other four centre-backs ahead of him: Chelsea's Gary Cahill, Manchester City's John Stones, and Manchester United's Phil Jones and Chris Smalling.

All four were top defenders at Champions League clubs, but Harry was as fearless as ever.

'Let the battles begin!' he told himself.

It was a sharp learning curve for Harry. He was playing at the very highest level now. He listened carefully to all the advice he received, especially from his manager. Southgate had played fifty-seven times for England as a centre-back. He knew what he was talking about when it came to international defending!

In the end, Harry didn't make his debut against Malta or Slovakia. Instead, he watched from the bench as Gary and Phil led England to victory. He wasn't too disappointed, though – he returned to

Leicester feeling more motivated than ever. He was nearly there! One month later, he was called up again.

'Nice new suitcase, H!' Jordan teased. 'They must be paying you well at Leicester!'

Harry Kane's late winner against Slovenia meant that England were through to the World Cup with one game to spare! That was especially good news for Harry because Southgate now had the chance to try something new.

'We're going to play a back three against Lithuania,' his manager explained, 'and I want you to play on the left.'

Harry couldn't believe it – he was in the England starting line-up!

Once he had recovered from the shock, he thanked his three Hull managers: Bruce, Phelan and Silva. They were the ones who had spotted his potential as the ball player in a back three. And, of course, his friend Andrew. Without him at left-back, Harry's job would have been so much harder.

'Good luck, mate!' Andrew messaged back,

followed by a Scottish flag emoji.

The LFF Stadium in Vilnius wasn't exactly Wembley, but Harry didn't care. He would have happily made his England senior debut in front of one man and his dog!

As the match against Lithuania kicked off, he was more excited than nervous. He tried to treat it like any other of the hundreds of games that he had played.

In the fourth minute, he had the perfect chance to make it a dream debut. Aaron Cresswell's cross was perfect, right on his big head. Somehow, however, he missed the ball completely.

'Noooo!' Harry groaned. He was usually so good in the air.

But instead of dwelling on his mistake, he kept going. England were dominating the game, so Harry did what he did best – attack from the back!

In the twenty-sixth minute, he chipped a clever ball through to Jordan, who headed it back into Dele's path. As Dele ran onto it, a defender fouled him. Penalty!

'Great ball, H!' Jordan called out, giving him a big thumbs-up.

Phew! He had made up for his earlier error. England's other Harry – Harry Kane – scored from the spot. 1–0!

That turned out to be the final score. As he shook hands with the Lithuania players, Harry felt happy with his first England performance. One game, one cleansheet! Apart from that missed header, he had looked comfortable and composed throughout. But had he done enough to keep his place against tougher opponents?

Harry would have to wait and see. In the meantime, he enjoyed his big moment. After years of being England's biggest fan, he was now an England player! Once his teammates had signed his shirt, he framed it and hung it proudly on his wall at home.

'You never know – that might be my only cap!' he told his girlfriend, Fern.

It wasn't, though. In November 2017, Harry played ninety minutes against Germany and then ninety minutes against Brazil. Battling with the best

attackers in the world, he was as solid as a rock
in England's back three. Three games, three clean
sheets!

'I just stopped Neymar from scoring!' Harry
laughed.

Sometimes, he had to pinch himself to make sure
that he wasn't dreaming. With the 2018 World Cup
only months away, Harry was now one of England's
first-choice centre-backs. He just had to keep playing
well, and keep believing.

CHAPTER 22

LEICESTER'S NEW LEADER

It was turning into a whirlwind season for Harry. Four days after keeping Neymar quiet at Wembley, he was back in the Premier League, with Leicester, taking on Pep Guardiola's awesome Manchester City attack. For forty-five minutes, Leicester's defence held on.

'Keep concentrating!' Harry shouted to his teammates. He was one of their leaders already.

Raheem Sterling played a one-two with Kevin De Bruyne, and then slipped a pass through to David Silva, who quickly crossed to Gabriel Jesus. 1–0!

As the ball rolled past Kasper Schmeichel, Harry kicked the air in frustration. Leicester had been beaten by a magical City move but it was still disappointing. These days, Harry felt every goal he conceded like a punch in the gut. He wanted to be the best defender in the world!

'Next time,' Harry muttered to himself. That was the good thing about playing game after game. He always had the chance to learn from his mistakes. Ten days later, Leicester beat Tottenham 2–1. In the battle of England's 'Harrys', Maguire defeated Kane.

Leicester changed their manager – Claude Puel replaced Craig Shakespeare – but the team tactics stayed the same. With two defensive midfielders protecting him, Harry had the freedom to attack from the back.

'Go!' Claude Puel told him, pointing towards the opposition half.

Against Southampton, Harry chested the ball down in the penalty area, turned and then fired a dangerous ball across goal. Andy King was there for a tap-in at the back post. 3–1 to Leicester!

'Cheers, H!'

Against Manchester United, Leicester were losing 2–1 with seconds to go. As Marc Albrighton curled one last ball into the box, Harry made his trademark dash towards the back post. His England teammates Phil Jones and Chris Smalling watched the cross sail over their heads and thought it was going out for a goal kick.

How wrong they were! Harry stretched out his long right leg and coolly volleyed the ball past the goalkeeper.

Goooooooooooooooooooaaaaaaaaaaaaaaalllllllllllll llllllllllllll!!!!!!!!!!!!!!!!!!!

Harry was Leicester's last-minute hero! He ran past the club mascot, Filbert Fox, and slid on his knees in front of the delighted fans. There was no better feeling in the whole of football.

Harry Maguire! Harry Maguire!

'What a finish!' Shinji shouted.

Harry was dominating in defence too. Training against Jamie every week was tough, but it made him a better player. As a defender, he faced lots of different challenges. With his height and strength, he could battle with the big boys like Lukaku and Costa all game long.

It was the smaller, speedier strikers that caused him more problems. Jamie was one of the quickest players Harry had ever seen. In order to stop him, Harry had to be alert all the time, looking out for signs of danger. Their battles were fierce and full of banter.

'How many have you scored today, Vards?' he asked.

'Shut up, Slabhead! How many Premier League titles have you won?'

Harry was loving life at Leicester. Robert still wasn't back from injury, so he played game after game, in the Premier League, the League Cup *and* the FA Cup. Harry even played twice against his old club, Sheffield United. It was a nice reminder of how far he had come.

'Don't overdo it!' his mum warned him. 'Remember, you've got the World Cup coming up this summer.'

'I know, I can rest when I've retired!' Harry replied.

He had to keep playing. Every header, block, tackle and interception was taking him one step closer to Southgate's final squad for the tournament in Russia.

Harry started on the bench in England's next friendly against the Netherlands but he didn't stay there long. Joe Gomez got injured in the tenth minute and Harry ran on to replace him.

England had an all-Yorkshire back three now: Kyle Walker on the right, John Stones in the middle and Harry on the left. Kyle was from Sheffield, and he had been a couple of years ahead of Harry at United.

'The Maguire Boys!' he remembered with a grin. 'Yeah, I used to hear lots of good things about you guys!'

John, meanwhile, was born just up the road in Barnsley.

'I started out in the Tykes academy,' Harry explained excitedly. 'Maybe we met when we were younger, Stonesy!'

'I doubt it, mate. I wouldn't forget a big head like yours!'

Between the three of them, Kyle, John and Harry had so much strength, skill and speed. The poor Dutch attackers had no chance.

The match finished England 1 Netherlands 0. Four games, four clean sheets!

Fingers crossed, Harry had done enough to earn a World Cup place. There was no time to worry, though. Four days after returning to Leicester, Harry was too busy beating Brighton.

In the end, the Foxes finished ninth in the Premier League and reached the quarter finals of both cups. It had been an acceptable campaign for Leicester but an exceptional one for their new young leader at the back.

At the club's end of season ceremony, Harry won both the Players' Player and Player of the Year awards. He'd achieved this at three clubs – first Sheffield United, then Hull City, and now Leicester City!

The audience clapped and cheered as Harry walked onto the stage, dressed in a smart navy suit. It made a change from his usual club tracksuit! Everyone agreed that he was a worthy winner. He had been Leicester's Mr Consistent, playing every single minute of every single Premier League match.

'I'm really honoured to collect these awards,' he said humbly. 'I've been really lucky to come to this club. There's a great bunch of lads here and a great team spirit. The supporters have been brilliant with me ever since I joined. So thank you, and let's hope we can win a few trophies next season!'

Before that, however, Harry was hoping to win a trophy for his country. On 16 May, Southgate announced his England squad for the 2018 World Cup.

The FA released a video where each player's name was revealed one by one. Raheem Sterling was first, then John Stones, then Trent Alexander-Arnold. Eventually, the camera zoomed in on a tall grey tower block where a girl and a boy were holding up a big white banner. They yelled the two words written there at the tops of their voices:

'HARRY MAGUIRE!'

'Yes, Big Man!' Jamie messaged. He was in the squad too. 'Russia, here we come!'

CHAPTER 23

WORLD CUP 2018

Being selected for England's 2018 World Cup squad was a huge achievement for Harry. However, his ambition didn't stop there. He wanted to start every single match for his country, just like he did for his club. Kyle Walker and John Stones were guaranteed to play but Harry was battling with Gary Cahill for that final place in the back three.

'Cahill's won two Premier League titles *and* the Champions League!' his brothers told him, hoping to fire Harry up. The whole Maguire family was heading out to Russia to cheer him on.

Yes, Gary was certainly the more experienced option. He had fifty-nine England caps, whereas

Harry only had four. However, if Southgate wanted someone who could bring the ball out of defence, Harry was his man!

In England's last two warm-up matches, Gary played against Nigeria and then Harry played against Costa Rica. Gary scored in a 2–1 win, and then Harry kept a clean sheet in a 2–0 win. Before the first group game against Tunisia, Southgate had a big decision to make.

In the meantime, the England players settled into their World Cup base camp in Repino. They were miles away from the capital city, Moscow, and Harry was expecting to be really bored. But instead, he had loads of fun!

When training ended, there were lots of different activities for the players to do together: Fortnite, basketball, pool. When Jamie wanted to play table tennis, he knew who to ask.

'Fancy a game, Big H?'

'Sure, Vards, as long as you're ready for another thrashing!'

It all helped to build a really strong team spirit.

During the Premier League season, they competed against each other for their clubs but this was different. For the World Cup, they were united, competing together for their country.

After weeks of watching and thinking, Southgate picked Harry to play in England's first match against Tunisia. When he heard the great news, he wanted to slide across the grass on his knees. Harry couldn't wait!

The Three Lions started brilliantly. They could have been 2–0 up after ten minutes! Instead, however, it was still 0–0 as Harry went forward for the corner. Ashley Young delivered a deep cross towards England's big men and John headed it goalwards. The Tunisia keeper made a super save but Harry Kane was in the right place for the rebound. 1–0!

All the players piled on top of each other in a happy team bundle. As a big centre-back, Harry had to be careful not to hurt anyone.

'Sorry!' he shouted sheepishly to Raheem.

England were in total control until the thirty-fifth minute. Suddenly, a cross came in and Kyle fouled the Tunisia striker. Penalty – 1–1!

It was a cruel blow but the England players didn't panic. There was plenty of time left to grab another goal.

Harry did what he did best – attack from the back! In the second half, he played like an extra midfielder. He dribbled forward into space, looking for a killer pass. Harry had more touches on the ball than any of his teammates, but with seconds to go, the score was still 1–1.

Corner-kick! Harry rushed forward to attack Kieran Trippier's cross. It was now or never. *BOOM!* He jumped high to win the header. Harry Kane was in the right place again to steer the ball home. 2–1!

The two Harrys were the England heroes! It was an amazing moment that neither of them would ever forget. In their first-ever World Cup match, with the hopes of a nation resting on their shoulders, they had saved the day.

'Nice one, Slabhead!' Jamie shouted as the whole squad celebrated in front of the relieved and jubilant fans.

It was the start of an exciting new era for England. After years of misery and frustration, the nation had finally found another team of fearless footballers.

Back home, the hope was building but at the England base camp, it was all fun and games. The players relaxed by racing inflatable unicorns in the swimming pool.

'Where's the VAR when you need it?' Kyle joked.

A few days later, Harry was answering questions from the media, when a familiar face snuck into the room.

'It's Jamie Vardy here from Vardy News,' he said, pretending that his fist was a microphone. 'Just how big is the diameter of your head?'

'Good one, Vards!' Harry thought to himself. Now his big head was all anyone wanted to talk about.

England's next match against Panama was a whole lot easier. Thanks to goals from John, Jesse Lingard and Harry Kane, they were 5–0 up by half-time! The Three Lions were through to the Round of 16.

Even a 1–0 loss to Belgium couldn't dampen their spirits. England hadn't won a World Cup knock-out match since 2006, but that was all about to change against Colombia. The whole country believed.

'Three Lions on a shirt!' Joe and Laurence Maguire sang along with the rest of the supporters in Moscow. This time, their brother wasn't with them; Harry was out there playing on the pitch instead!

And what a game he was having. At the heart of the England defence, Harry won header after header. It was an angry, competitive match but there was nothing he liked more than a battle.

When Harry Kane scored a penalty, it looked like they were through to the quarter-finals. In the last minute, however, Yerry Mina equalised for Colombia.

The England fans fell silent. Could their warriors keep fighting, or was it game over? Harry certainly wasn't giving up.

'Come on, lads!' he clapped and cheered. 'We can do this!'

Together, the team held on through the thirty minutes of extra-time. Penalties!

'Oh no!' the fans groaned.

England had never won a World Cup shoot-out. They had lost against West Germany in 1990, against Argentina in 1998, and against Portugal in 2006. On top of all that, there were the losses against Germany in Euro 96, against Portugal in Euro 2004, and against Italy in Euro 2012.

As England's biggest fan, Harry had seen a lot of failure. It was time for them to write a new story of success.

Even when Jordan Henderson's penalty was saved, Harry didn't give up hope.

Mateus Uribe stepped up and… hit the crossbar!

Carlos Bacca ran up and… Jordan Pickford made a super save!

Now, Eric Dier just needed to keep cool and…

Gooooooooooooooooooooaaaaaaaaaaaaaaaaaallllllllllll llllllllllllllllll!!!!!!!!!!!!!!!!!!

What a moment – England were through to the World Cup quarter-finals after WINNING ON PENALTIES! Harry was ecstatic as he raced over to join the big team bundle.

In the stands in Russia, and back in England, everyone was singing the same old tune:

It's coming home, it's coming home,
It's coming, FOOTBALL'S COMING HOME!

Was football really coming home? Suddenly, the impossible seemed possible.

'Good luck, Big H!' Andrew messaged him before the quarter-final, followed by a Scottish flag emoji.

His friend had just played in the Champions League final with Liverpool. Hull's two young signings had turned into superstars!

Sweden were the next team standing in England's way. It wouldn't be easy but Harry wasn't leaving the World Cup without an almighty fight.

In the thirtieth minute, Harry's thumping header gave England the lead.

Goooooooooooooooooooooaaaaaaaaaaaaaaaalllllllllllll lllllllllllllll!!!!!!!!!!!!!!!!!!!!

What a time to score his first international goal! Harry raced towards the fans, pumping his fists and roaring like a lion. His country meant so much to him.

Sixty long minutes later, England were through to the World Cup semi-finals! It was an incredible achievement for such a young, inexperienced group of players. Of all the new national heroes, Harry was now the biggest of them all.

First, there was the song:

Harry Maguire, your defence is terrified!
Harry Maguire, na na na na na na na na na na!

Then, there were the memes. A funny photo of Harry talking to Fern after the Colombia match exploded on to the Internet. Everyone was adding their own comedy captions, including Harry himself:

'Can you ask the neighbours to put the bins out on Monday?' he wrote after the Sweden win. 'We're not going home just yet!'

That was one of the many things that the England fans loved about Harry; he was just so normal and down to earth. Despite becoming a World Cup hero, he was keeping his feet firmly on the ground. Ahead of the semi-final, he took part in a fun darts challenge.

'Good luck, Harry!' the fans cheered for their favourite.

He won, of course! Harry was a natural, all-round sportsman. After shaking hands, he went back to focusing on football.

Against Croatia in the semi-final, England got off to an amazing start. In the fifth minute, Kieran curled a free-kick into the top corner. 1–0!

It's coming home, it's coming home,
It's coming, FOOTBALL'S COMING HOME!

No, Harry knew that England weren't in the final yet. There was lots of defending left to do. The back three battled hard, winning headers, tackles and interceptions.

Kyle, John and Harry – they were a brave band of superheroes.

'Nothing's getting past us!'

In the second half, however, Croatia fought back fiercely. They attacked again and again until finally they scored. 1–1!

Could England hold strong? Harry did his best but the whole team was so tired. Deep in extra-time, Mario Mandžuki grabbed the winning goal. As Harry watched the ball cross the line, he had that horrible sinking feeling once again. England were out of the World Cup.

Harry was very disappointed but it wasn't all doom and gloom. No-one had expected them to get so far in the tournament. The players had made their country very proud. Harry and his England teammates stood together on the pitch, thanking the fans with their heads held high.

'This is just the beginning, boys!' Gareth Southgate promised.

Harry hoped so. He really didn't want his amazing football adventure to end. It was hard to believe how far he had come already.

After starting out with Sheffield United, Harry had risen higher and higher, step by step, game after game, through ups and downs, highs and lows. League One, then the Championship, then the Premier League – and now the World Cup.

Through hard work, belief and dedication, Harry and his big head had conquered them all.

Turn the page for a sneak preview of
another brilliant football story by
Matt and Tom Oldfield. . .

KANE

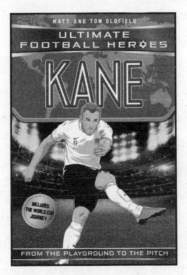

Available now!

CHAPTER 1

ENGLAND HERO

Thursday, 5 October 2017

In the Wembley tunnel, Harry closed his eyes and soaked up the amazing atmosphere. He was back at the home of football, the stadium where he had first achieved his childhood dream of playing for England. 19 March 2015, England vs Lithuania – he remembered that game like it was yesterday. He had scored that day and now, with England facing Slovenia, he needed to do it again. As England's captain and Number 9, it was his job to shoot them to the 2018 World Cup.

'Come on, lads!' Harry called out to his teammates behind him, friends like Joe Hart, Kyle Walker and

Eric Dier. It was a real honour to be their leader. With a victory over Slovenia, they would all be on their way to the biggest tournament of their lives in Russia.

Harry looked down at the young mascot by his side and smiled at him. 'Right, let's do this!'

As the two of them led the England team out on to the pitch, the fans clapped and cheered. Harry didn't look up at the thousands of faces and flags; instead, he looked down at the grass in front of him. He was totally focused on his task: scoring goals and beating Slovenia.

'If you get a chance, test the keeper,' Harry said to his partners in attack, Raheem Sterling and Marcus Rashford, before kick-off. 'I'll be there for the rebound!'

Harry's new Premiereship season with Tottenham Hotspur had not begun well in August, but by September he was back to his lethal best. That month alone, he scored an incredible 13 goals, including two goals for England against Malta. He could score every type of goal – tap-ins, headers, one-on-ones, long-range shots, penalties, even free kicks. That's what made him such a dangerous striker.

With Slovenia defending well, Harry didn't get many chances in the first half. He got in good positions but the final ball never arrived.

'There's no need to panic yet,' Harry told his teammates in the dressing room. He really didn't want a repeat of England's terrible performance against Iceland at Euro 2016. That match still haunted him. 'We're good enough to win this by playing our natural game. Be patient!'

As Ryan Bertrand dribbled down the left wing, Harry sprinted towards the six-yard box. Ryan's cross didn't reach him but the ball fell to Raheem instead. His shot was going in until a defender deflected it wide.

'Unlucky!' Harry shouted, putting his hands on his head. 'Keep going, we're going to score!'

Without this kind of strong self-belief, Harry would never have made it to the top of European football. There had been lots of setbacks along the way: rejections, disappointments and bad form. But every time, Harry bounced back with crucial goals at crucial moments. That's what made him such a superstar.

A matter of seconds later, a rebound fell to him on the edge of the penalty area. Surely, this was his moment. He pulled back his left foot and curled a powerful shot towards the bottom corner. The fans were already up on their feet, ready to celebrate. Harry never missed… but this time he did. The ball flew just wide of the post. Harry couldn't believe it. He looked up at the sky and sighed.

On the sideline, England manager Gareth Southgate cheered his team on. 'That's much better – the goal is coming, lads!'

But after ninety minutes, the goal still hadn't come. The fourth official raised his board: eight minutes of injury time.

'It's not over yet, boys!' Harry shouted, to inspire his teammates.

The Slovenian goalkeeper tried to throw the ball out to his left-back but Kyle got there first. Straight away, Harry was on the move from the back post to the front post. After playing together for years at Tottenham, they knew how to score great goals.

As Kyle crossed it in, Harry used his burst of speed to get in front of the centre-back. Again, the England supporters stood and waited anxiously. The ball was perfect and Harry stretched out his long right leg to meet it. The keeper got a touch on his shot but he couldn't keep it out.

Goooooooooooooaaaaaaaaaaaaaaaaaaaaalllllllllllllllllllll llllll!!!!!!!!!!!!!!!!!!!!!

He had done it! Joy, relief, pride – Harry felt every emotion as he ran towards the fans. This time, he hadn't let them down. He held up the Three Lions on his shirt and screamed until his throat got sore.

'Captain to the rescue!' Kyle laughed as they hugged by the corner flag.

'No, it was all thanks to you!' Harry replied.

At the final whistle, he threw his arms up in the air. It was a phenomenal feeling to qualify for the 2018 World Cup. He couldn't wait to lead England to glory.

'We are off to Russia!' a voice shouted over the

loudspeakers and the whole stadium cheered.

It was yet another moment that Harry would never forget. Against the odds, he was making his childhood dreams come true. He was the star striker for Tottenham, the club that he had supported all his life. And now, like his hero David Beckham, he was the captain of England.

Harry had never given up, even when it looked like he wouldn't make it as a professional footballer. With the support of his family and his coaches, and lots of hard work and dedication, he had proved everyone wrong to become a world-class goal machine.

It had been an incredible journey from Walthamstow to Wembley, and Harry was only just getting started.

HARRY MAGUIRE
HONOURS

Hull City

🏆 Football League Championship Play-Offs: 2015–16

Individual

🏆 PFA League One Team of the Year: 2011–12,
2012–13, 2013–14

🏆 Sheffield United Player of the Year: 2011–12,
2012–13, 2013–14

🏆 Hull City Fans' Player of the Year: 2016–17

🏆 Hull City Players' Player of the Year: 2016–17

🏆 Leicester City Player of the Season: 2017–18

🏆 Leicester City Players' Player of the Season:
2017–18

MAGUIRE

15 & 6

THE FACTS

NAME: JACOB HARRY MAGUIRE

DATE OF BIRTH: 5 March 1993

AGE: 25

PLACE OF BIRTH: Sheffield

NATIONALITY: England

BEST FRIEND: Jamie Vardy

CURRENT CLUB: Leicester City

POSITION: CB

THE STATS

Height (cm):	**194**
Club appearances:	**301**
Club goals:	**18**
Club trophies:	**1**
International appearances:	**12**
International goals:	**0**
International trophies:	**0**
Ballon d'Ors:	**0**

★ ★ ★ **HERO RATING: 82** ★ ★ ★

GREATEST MOMENTS

Type and search the web links to see the magic for yourself!

1 ★ 4 JANUARY 2014, ASTON VILLA 1–2 SHEFFIELD UNITED

https://www.youtube.com/watch?v=cIGWwAvkiSI
Harry was already playing game after game in League One but this FA Cup run gave him the chance to battle with the big boys. At Villa Park, he took on Christian Benteke, one of the strongest strikers in the Premier League, and won! After that, Harry knew that he could play at the highest level.

2 — 28 MAY 2016,
HULL CITY 1–0 SHEFFIELD WEDNESDAY

https://www.youtube.com/watch?v=qBcqIQ9-TzM

Harry was only on the pitch for the final five minutes of this play-off final but it was still a massive moment for him. After two relegations and two play-off failures, he won promotion at last! Best of all, it gave Harry his second shot at playing in the Premier League.

3 — 5 APRIL 2017,
HULL CITY 4–2 MIDDLESBROUGH

https://www.youtube.com/watch?v=FA7n5TRqHwA

Marco Silva almost pulled off the miracle of keeping Hull in the Premier League. Harry was Silva's leader on the pitch and he saved his best performance for this epic relegation battle. First, Harry set up Abel Hernández with a perfect pass and then he scored a goal of his own.

4   23 DECEMBER 2017, LEICESTER CITY 2–2 MANCHESTER UNITED

https://www.youtube.com/watch?v=1BwcWeNdnJ4
It didn't take Harry long to become a Leicester leader after his big-money move. The Foxes were losing 2–1 to Manchester United with seconds to go, when up popped Harry, at the back post as usual. He stretched out his long right leg and coolly volleyed the ball past the goalkeeper.

5   9 JULY 2018, SWEDEN 0–2 ENGLAND

https://www.youtube.com/watch?v=yMloUtQRHos
Harry was already an England World Cup hero but, in the quarter-final, he became a superhero! In the 30th minute, he muscled his way past the Sweden defenders and powered a thumping header into the bottom corner. 1–0! And England were on their way to the semi-finals!

PLAY LIKE YOUR HEROES

THE HARRY MAGUIRE THUMPING HEADER

SEE IT HERE You Tube

https://www.youtube.com/watch?v=L7qSFd6YyYo

STEP 1: When your team wins a corner, make your way forward. This is your big moment!

Step 2: Stop on the edge of the penalty area. You can have a little chat with your teammates if you like because…

Step 3: …You want to leave it as late as possible before making your run. That way, you catch your marker by surprise!

Step 4: Muscle your way through the defence. Don't let anything stop you.

Step 5: Aim for a corner. Top or bottom, left or right – just make your header impossible to save! GOAL!

Step 6: Run towards your fans, roaring like the lion you are.

TEST YOUR KNOWLEDGE

QUESTIONS

1. What was the name of Harry's first football club?

2. What was Harry's first position on the football pitch?

3. Who did Harry's Sheffield United face in the 2011 FA Youth Cup Final?

4. Harry played for the England Under-21s – true or false?

5. How old was Harry when he made his 100th start for Sheffield United?

6. Which other young star joined Hull City on the same day as Harry?

7. Which club did Harry join on loan in 2015?

8. Who did Harry replace in the Leicester City defence?

9. How many games did Harry miss during the 2017-18 Premier League season?

10. Who were England's opponents when Harry made his senior international debut?

11. Who gave Harry the nickname 'Slabhead'?

Answers below. . . No cheating!

The 2018 World Cup saw England's young lions produce their best performance for a generation, and storm to the semi-finals of the World Cup.

Complete your collection with these international edition Ultimate Football Heroes.